D0983998

Hand-Stitched
Home

THE CURIOUS GARDENER   ANNA PAVORD

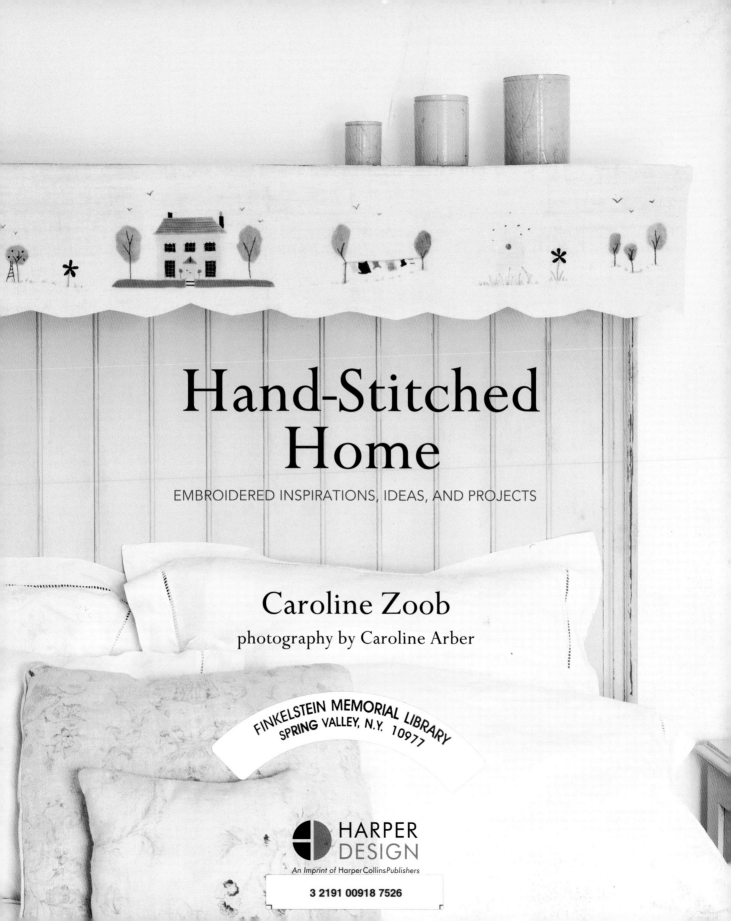

Hand-Stitched Home

EMBROIDERED INSPIRATIONS, IDEAS, AND PROJECTS

Caroline Zoob

photography by Caroline Arber

FINKELSTEIN MEMORIAL LIBRARY
SPRING VALLEY, N.Y. 10977

3 2191 00918 7526

Harper
DESIGN

An Imprint of HarperCollinsPublishers

*To Caroline Turner and Miranda Money
for their unfailing friendship and support*

Hand-Stitched Home
Text and projects copyright © 2013 by
Caroline Zoob
Design, photography, artwork, and layout
copyright © 2013 by Jacqui Small

All rights reserved. No part of this book
may be used or reproduced in any manner
whatsoever without written permission
except in the case of brief quotations
embodied in critical articles and reviews.
Reproduction of the projects inside may
not be used for commercial purposes. For
information, address Harper Design, 10 East
53rd Street, New York, NY 10022.

HarperCollins books may be purchased
for educational, business, or sales
promotional use. For information, please
write: Special Markets Department,
HarperCollinsPublishers, 10 East 53rd
Street, New York, NY 10022.

Published in 2013 by:
Harper Design
An Imprint of HarperCollins*Publishers*
10 East 53rd Street
New York, NY 10022
Tel (212) 207-7000
harperdesign@harpercollins.com
www.harpercollins.com

Distributed throughout the world by:
HarperCollinsPublishers
10 East 53rd Street
New York, NY 10022

Library of Congress Control Number:
2013930933

ISBN: 978-0-06225004-9

Printed in China, 2013

Contents

Left: A vintage director's chair has been given new life with chair backs made from antique French linen, decorated with a simple stylized white flower appliquéd to one side.

Opposite: Three small whitework flowers along the edge of the seat of this antique French chair echo the carved decoration on the back of the chair and introduce an embroidered touch to an otherwise austere room.

Introduction

Man is primed to want to decorate a blank surface, whether by placing handprints on the walls of Neolithic caves or by embroidering linen burial cloths for the mummified dead in the Egypt of 2000 BC. The Book of Exodus in the Bible is full of references to embroidery.

Little domestic embroidery survives from before the fifteenth century, and yet it is not hard to imagine that it was used to decorate and add comfort in the simplest of homes for many centuries before.

Today many people associate embroidery in the home with the piles of embroidered tray cloths, doilies, and antimacassars made from patterns published in women's magazines in the first half of the twentieth century. Today our interiors are simpler, yet there is still a place for embroidered detail. It can be as simple as a white flower on the edge of an upholstered chair or a line of running stitch along the edge of a stripe. Conversely, a sparely furnished room with a neutral color palette can be transformed by one or two richly embroidered surfaces. The aim of this book is to suggest ways in which you can add embroidered detail to your home, whatever your personal decorating style may be.

Left: An arrangement of garden flowers in my workroom ready for sketching.

Opposite: A collection of laces, threads, buttons, and fabric is gathered in preparation for starting a new piece.

Inspiration
When you decorate a room you gather swatches of fabric, scraps of carpet, little cards of paint colors to set the tone for how you want the room to look. You should also do this when you are thinking of starting an embroidery. Collect materials that will inspire a beautiful design, such as threads, buttons, little frames, old greetings cards and scraps of lace. Keep them around you when you begin to plan how you want your work to look. What works for me is to always have a row of little bottles on my workroom windowsill, in which I display flowers or leaves on stems. The more you surround yourself with pretty colors, textures, and natural finds, the easier you will find it to embroider. Most important of all though is to keep your eyes open to spot the things around you that you can visualize captured in stitches.

Left: Ready-made trims such as this vintage French piping are useful for projects such as the embroidered pelmet on page 116. There are replicas available in a variety of colors.

Opposite, clockwise from top left: You can find sections of lace at vintage fairs or online. Even the smallest of pieces can be reworked into something lovely; Hanks of handspun linen thread could be embroidered on an open-weave base fabric; A pile of antique linen sheets in various shades of white and buff; Vintage linen threads. Stitching in coarser linen thread gives a more organic, natural look which works well in contemporary interiors.

Material

The choice of fabric on which to embroider is very important. I have to confess here a love of antique French linen sheets: from the fine ones with their immaculate monograms worked by nuns to the rough hemp ones with their subtle, slubby weaves. The colors of the sheets vary hugely and they are never truly white. Very often the color and texture of a piece of old linen will be enough to inspire a particular embroidery, such as happened with the bedhead pelmet on page 58.

Not everyone has access to antique linen. If you are buying new fabric, try to find a fabric with a bit of life and texture to it. Many of the fabric houses have started to produce lightweight linens designed to have the look and feel of old fabric, and these are wonderful for embroidery. If you have to use new fabric, wash it at the hottest temperature recommended to pre-shrink it; there is nothing worse than washing your finished work and finding that the material shrinks and your embroidery does not.

Collecting fabric for appliqué

I consider appliqué to be a form of embroidery and for this technique it is really important to collect as many scraps as you can. Before you give clothes away, think about whether they might not be useful for appliqué. Tell friends that you are collecting fabrics. Remember that the tiniest scraps could work, and the more worn and faded the fabric, the better. It is a good idea to sort them by color/type: red checks, blue stripes, solids, etc. Sometimes you might find fabric in the most unexpected places: for example, the little piece of folded linen in the picture on page 15 was the selvage from a piece of nineteenth-century beige-and-ivory ticking I found at a flea market.

Having your own workroom is a luxury, but if you cannot set aside an entire room try to have a closet or set of drawers where you can keep your fabrics and threads in order. The compartmentalized containers sold in hardware shops are useful for this.

Right: I should keep my colors in the order of the color wheel, but I do not and sometimes this results in an unexpectedly happy juxtaposition of colors, which might in turn remind me of a piece of fabric I have tucked away—and suddenly a new piece starts to ferment.

Opposite: A drawer full of antique French mattress tickings, so called because the tight weave kept the ticks out. With their strong weaves and faded colors, and endless variations on a striped theme, they can be used to offset embroidery, or decorated with stitching.

Colors

A recent television documentary I watched claimed that no two people see color in the same way. Color is all important in embroidery. The finest stitching in the world will be off-putting if done in garish colors. This is one of the problems with all those dish towels and chair protectors from the 1930s: the curious predilection for combining lilac, orange, ultramarine, bright yellow, and cerise with greenery veering more to the turquoise than the lovely yellowy greens of nature. Very occasionally you find one of these cloths where either the colors have faded over the years, or, even better, the embroiderer eschewed the recommended colors and went off on a frolic of her own, using more subtle colors.

When you start an embroidery, after you have chosen your base cloth, lay out your threads and select the colors. Have the confidence to follow your own preferences. This is one reason why I have not given specific thread color references in this book. One tip when buying embroidery threads: look at them in the natural light. For some reason sewing supply stores are given to burying their carousels of threads in the deepest recesses of their shops, and as the poet Elizabeth Barrett Browning said, "Colors seen by candle-light will not look the same by day." For this reason,

Left: I cannot leave little twists of vintage silk thread on a market stall. They simply have to come home and reside in my silks tin, next to my French antique collar box of wools. I love to rummage through them when starting a new piece to find the right color, and often use both for mood boards when I am working on a commercial project. Some of the vintage thread is impossibly fine but lovely to use for quilting or tiny stab stitches to add texture.

also, while you might only have time to embroider at night, choose your colors in the daylight hours. There is nothing worse than discovering that you have embroidered half your picture using a different green from the one you started with because when rooting around in your work basket in artificial light it was difficult to tell the difference.

If you are new to embroidering, the following is a list of basic colors to get you started:

Red: one tomato, one raspberry
Blue: one deep, one light gray-blue
Brown
Yellow: daisy-center yellow
Ivory
Green: at least two—see *A note about greens* opposite

A note about greens

Green is my favorite color. It is also one of the hardest colors to get right in embroidery. It will help if you remember how much yellow there is in the greens of nature. If you are embroidering a tree, mix two or three different greens together, making sure at least one of them has yellow undertones, so you get the effect of broken color and the result will look more natural. And always use a lighter green for the grass under the trees than the leaves on the tree to reflect the myriad of greens in nature.

If you are creating a deliberately stylized design, then a slightly brighter green, similar to the color of the large button in this picture, can work well. When in doubt, opt for a neutral green.

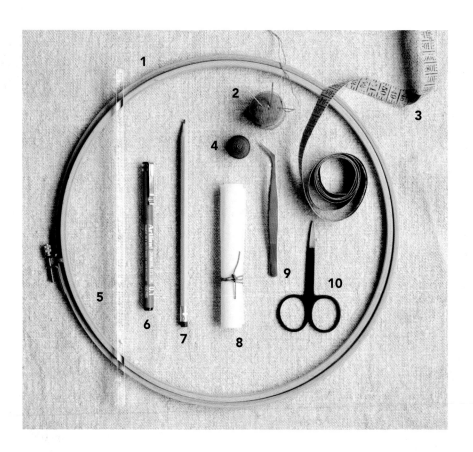

Left: Some of the vintage frames used for projects in this book.

Above right: A selection of useful tools which is by no means prescriptive: **1** Embroidery hoop **2** Pincushion and needles **3** Tape measure **4** Thimble **5** Clear acrylic ruler **6** Fine tipped art pen for sketching **7** Soft pencil for marking **8** Tracing paper for transferring patterns and templates **9** Craft tweezers **10** Small sharp scissors

Tools

There are not many tools required for hand embroidery, but these are what you need for the projects in the book. Some people prefer to use an embroidery hoop but generally I do not use one. It is of course important to have a selection of needles for different threads and fabrics. You will work more quickly if you thread up several needles with the different threads you plan to use and have them available on a large pincushion. A key tool is a pair of very sharp, small scissors. Do not use these for anything other than snipping your threads so they stay nice and sharp. I found the clear acrylic ruler and a long tweezers in an art shop, and have found them both invaluable. Use the rule to mark the fabric lightly when you have to keep your embroidery within a narrow parallel line. The tweezers are useful for placing small individual components of appliqué just before you press them to the base fabric. A thimble is useful if you are working with fabric with a dense weave. A good sharp pencil is essential for light marking on the base fabric. There are fading pens on the market, but I am wary of using them with antique fabrics. You will also need a basic sewing machine for appliqué and for sewing larger projects, such as cushions and window treatments.

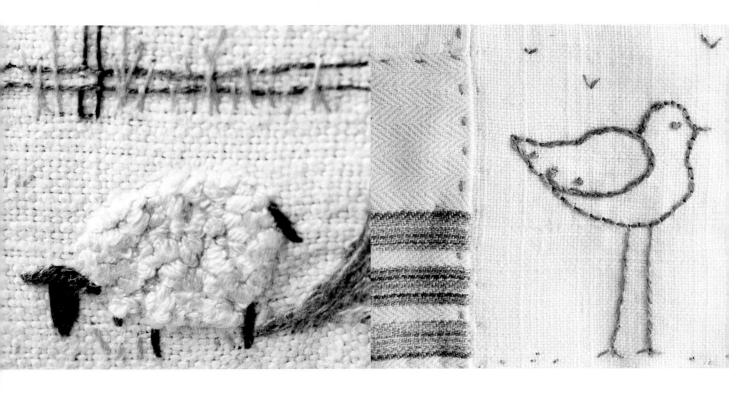

Making pictures

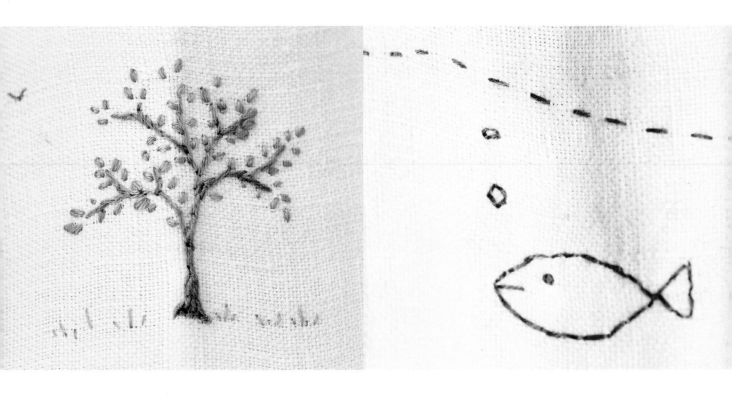

Inspired by the countryside

Is there an embroiderer who is not inspired by the countryside? Trees, flowers, animals, the patchwork patterns of fields and hedges—all lend themselves to embroidery. Roadside banks fringed with a mix of grass, Queen Anne's lace, poppies, cornflowers, and ox-eye daisies, the dip of a field outlined by post-and-rail fencing and little rows of trees breaking the line of a hillside—all of these cry out to be captured with the needle.

I once asked an artist where she found her inspiration and she told me it was simply a matter of keeping your eyes open. Nature is the richest source of inspiration, from the deceptive simplicity of the daisy to the intricacies of Queen Anne's lace or an allium gone to seed. Even if you do not plan to embroider a particular item, always bring home any interesting stems or seed heads you spot and keep them in a vase. It is also a good idea to keep a little notebook with you to jot down ideas or sketches. Gradually you will build up layers of inspiration so that when you pick up your needle everything will flow more easily.

Opposite: Propping these naïve embroideries on a table like decorative objects makes them work in a sophisticated interior setting better than if they were hung on the wall.

Inspiration from wild flowers

Gather drying flower heads in the fall so that you can study the underlying structure. I bought the vintage panel worked in wool (below right) because of its beautifully embroidered Queen Anne's lace.

Right: The frame suggests the embroidery. For this black-and-gilt frame, which was given to me to fill as a commission, I felt the formality of a standard daisy bush was appropriate. I lightly penciled the size of the circle but filled it without using tracings. The daisies are worked in three strands, but occasionally I gone doubled back to make the petals thicker. If you would like to embroider your own daisy basket, instructions are on pages 24 to 27.

Below: The gerbera lends itself to representation in stitches with its long petals in a collar around a lovely inflorescence.

Daisies are such cheerful flowers, reminiscent of summery days spent in fields making daisy chains. I have always loved them and almost the first thing I tried to embroider was a daisy. It is thought of as such a simple little flower and yet when you look closely at the layers of tiny petals joined to the central disk you appreciate that the structure is quite complicated. To begin with I embroidered them like sunflowers, or as a yellow face surrounded by straight white "lazy daisy" petals in a circle. Then one rainy day in Nice I came across an early study of marguerites by Matisse and noticed how he had captured all the different angles of the petals and the way that sometimes, when you look straight at a daisy, you only see the flat of the central disc and one or two petals sticking up at different angles. I began looking at daisies differently after I saw this painting, and I have tried ever since to make each daisy unique looking. Now I stitch the petals using long and short stitches built up in layers, which gives a more precise effect than simply using multistranded thread. For the centers, I sometimes use tiny stitches very close together, which more closely imitates the real structure of the flowers, or satin stitches pierced with a few tiny stab stitches.

Years ago at an antiques market I found an old basket with a slanted base that tilted slightly to one side. I took it home and filled it with a bunch of Michaelmas daisies and since then whenever I embroider a basket I have an image of it in my head. Have a look at the picture on page 22 of the little pot of daisies and you will see how they tilt at different angles. The larger the variety of flowers you include, the more movement your embroidery will contain. The embroidered daisy standard bush on page 23 is similar to this pot of flowers, but it has even more daisies.

Daisy basket picture

Materials

A frame—For me, the frame suggests the piece and certainly the base fabric.

Base fabric—Something fine in weave but still firm and not too textured. Also not too white so the daisies stand out.

Lining fabric

Threads

Bonding web

Muslin cloth

For the template for the embroidery see page 134

Stitches used:

Running stitch (see page 128)

Straight stitch (see page 128)

Rollover stitch (see page 131)

Satin stitch (see page 131)

Knot stitch (see page 131)

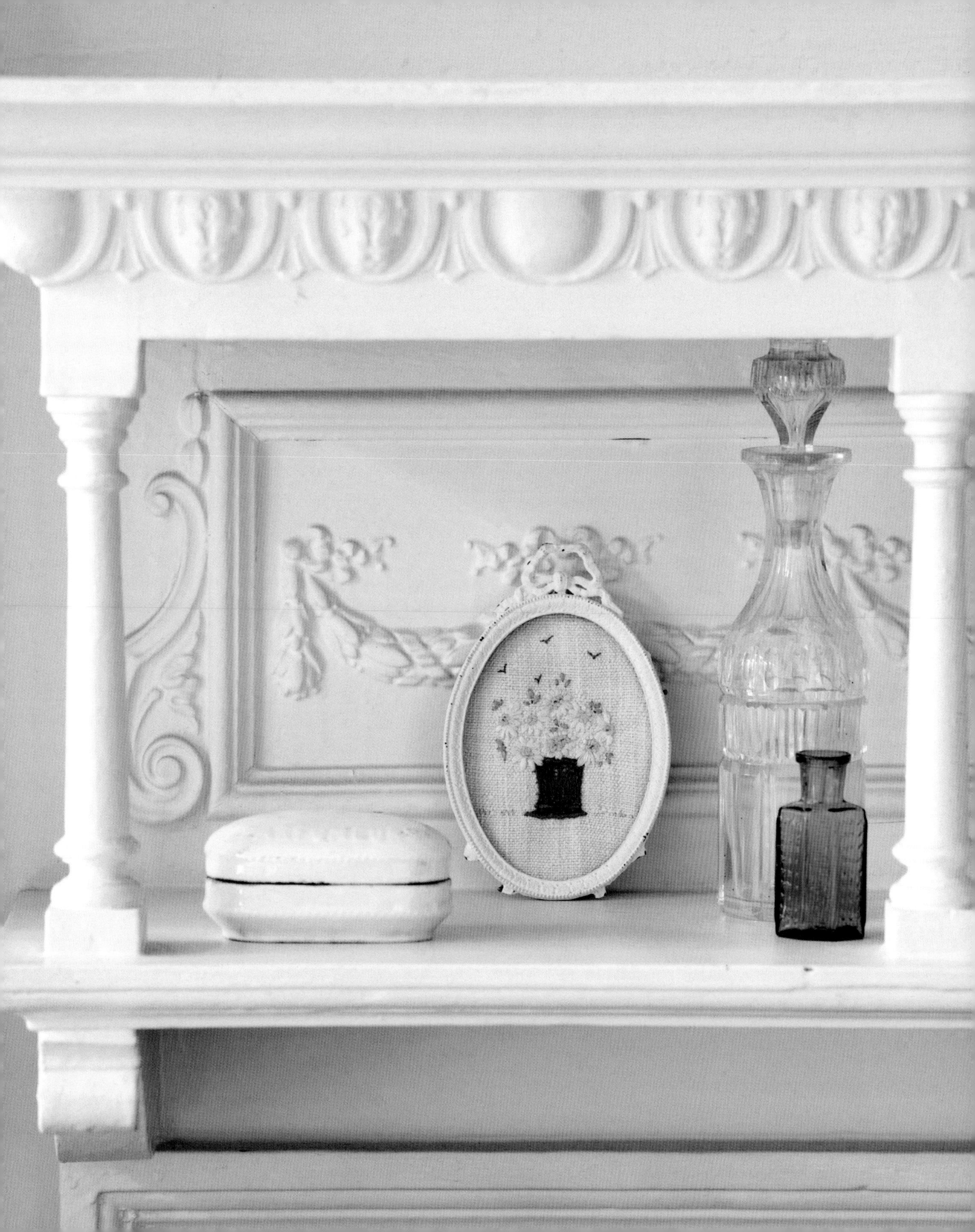

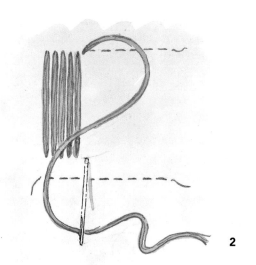

1

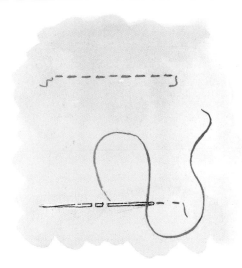

2

Method

1 First lay your frame wrong side up on the fabric with the glass out and mark where the corners are. Never work too close to the edge of the frame or your picture will look squashed in. Even in a small frame you want to have some space around your work. Decide where your ground level is and start to work the basket. First sew two lines of short running stitches as a guide for the top and bottom of your basket.

2 Using a single thread create the long vertical stitches to form the base of the basket. Keep the stitches close together and flat. Because they are long they may feel a little loose—don't worry about this. Create the flared base of the basket in the same away only using shorter stitches and have them on a slant.

3 Starting at the top, weave your needle and single thread in and out of each vertical stitch to the other side and then back. Repeat all the way to the base. It does not matter if you catch more than one thread occasionally as long as you create the woven effect. You will find that there is a slight pulling in at the sides of the basket—this is good as it makes the basket resemble a vase.

4 To create the lips that form the base of the basket and also its top edge, simply make three raised lines using a rollover stitch with double thread.

5

6

5 When you are happy with your basket, mark a single dot with a pencil wherever you want to have a daisy, and then begin to embroider the daisies. Start with the petals in straight stitch and fill in the centers later. Make sure you have at least one that falls over the front edge of the basket as in the picture. I worked these daisies in two strands and went over each petal twice. I prefer this technique to using four strands at once.

6 The centers of the daisies can be worked either in satin stitch or, as I have done here, knot stitch. When you are working the centers you can take the thread from one to the next, but always do a little back stitch on the wrong side of the one you are finishing and as you start the next. If you do this you will be able to snip the thread in between each flower. It might otherwise show through when you put everything together for framing.

7 When you have finished the daisies, add the little dots of green to balance everything out. I like to add flecks to suggest birds or insects above my embroideries because I think it adds movement or life to them, but this is optional.

8 Iron your embroidery through a muslin cloth. Trim any ends on the back so they do not show through. Cut a piece of bonding web the same size as the finished work. Fuse it to the back of the embroidery by following the manufacturer's instructions. Peel off the backing paper and lay the embroidery onto a lining fabric. Fuse the two pieces together with an iron. Press the front and trim to the exact size for your frame. The glass is the best template for this.

Sheep are great fun to embroider. Try sketching a few sheep to help you get started—the important thing to capture is the round wooliness of them and the way their ears stand apart from their faces at right angles. They are very forgiving subjects because the wool disguises their actual shape (unlike cows which are really hard to draw). When sheep are out in the fields at their most wooly, take some pictures so you can record how they gather together in little groups, some sitting, some standing, with the faces turned at different angles.

Sheep-and-tree bookends

Materials

A wooden block—This one was made of oak and was a 6-inch cube sawn in half diagonally. Oak is nice and heavy. You could have two cubes of wood if you prefer, and adapt the design for a square shape by putting the tree in the center.

Fabric to cover the bookends—I used antique French ticking in neutral colors as a contrast to the front.

Very light wadding

A staple gun

Threads

For the template for the embroidery see page 134

Stitches used:

Stem stitch (see page 129)

Split stitch (see page 129)

Straight stitch (see page 128)

Rollover stitch (see page 131)

Satin stitch (see page 131)

Knot stitch (see page 131)

Loopy stitch (see page 131)

Slip stich (see page 133)

Method

1 Prepare the block by stapling the wadding to it as neatly as possible.

2 Cut pieces of fabric for the face you plan to embroider and its opposite face, allowing $\frac{1}{2}$ inch extra all round. Staple the plain piece to the block though the wadding on the overlapping fabric, but not too close to the edge.

3 Fold the panel you are going to embroider over the block so you can mark the area of the embroidery. Do not embroider within $\frac{1}{4}$ inch of this fold to allow yourself a bit of leeway when fixing the panel to the block. Using the template lightly trace the fence onto the panel and stitch, followed by the tree. The fence is worked in single thread and you can use either stem, split, or straight stitches. Use a different brown for the fence than the one you use on the tree.

4 Now work the tree. I always start with the trunk, working a single thread in long and short stitches to give the effect of the bark. Flare the trunk out at the bottom, imagining as you do so the way that tree roots spread out and make the ground beneath them bumpy. Build the tree trunk and branches upward with satin stitch and knot stitch using single thread, and then use rollover stitch to create a few ridges in the bark. Add the leaves using stem stitch.

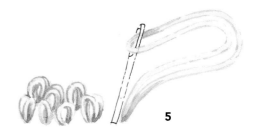

5

5 For the sheep I use four strands and make tiny stitches next to each other, but do not pull the thread tight to the fabric. You could use knot stitch, but I like using these loopy stitches as they feel a bit woolier. When you are happy with the body of the sheep, add their black faces, ears, feet, and tails.

6 Add blades of grass going across the legs of the sheep and the fence posts and some behind. Lastly, if you choose, add the little bird on the fence post.

7 Iron your embroidery. Staple it to the padded block. Cut a piece of fabric that will stretch around the long diagonal side and bottom of the block, allowing enough for a $\frac{1}{2}$ inch turn under on all edges. Slip stitch the fabric to the block, starting with the embroidered panel diagonal edge and continuing around, joining the two ends underneath the block as in the picture on the left. Alternatively, take the block, fabric, and embroidery to an upholsterer and ask him or her to do it for you!

These tiny embroidered hearts filled with lavender make charming decorative additions to keys, whether for a special box or the linen closet. You could personalize the heart with initials or a date, perhaps for keeping as sentimental family mementos.

This book is full of ideas for little motifs you could use. For instance, if you store your wine or china in a particular cabinet with a key, you could use the images from the pantry shelf edge project, or tie hearts with names onto baskets for shoes in the entryway.

Heart key fobs

Materials

Linen or other base cloth. Avoid anything too bulky or inflexible as the hearts are very small and therefore fiddly to turn out. You can use a contrasting cloth for the reverse if you prefer.

Fine string

Dried lavender

Threads for your chosen design

For the templates for the heart and embroidery see page 134

Stitches used:

The combination of stitches depends on your chosen design

Method

1 Choose your base cloth then make a template. A template made from stiff, clear plastic would be useful for this project, to help you make sure the embroidery fits into the heart. Embroider your design. Use the clear template to keep checking that the design will fit and avoid working too close to the edge.

2 Now use the clear template to ensure the design is centered correctly (place it over the reverse of your work) and draw around the template. Cut a second heart shape for the back. Pin the pieces, right sides together.

3 Stitch from position A to B on the template diagram. Try to follow the curved lines at the top of the heart slowly and precisely.

4 Clip the seams to the V of the heart and around the curves. Do not trim the heart—the seam allowance, as long as it is not too bulky, will actually help create the shape of the heart. Turn out, and fill with lavender. Slip stitch the opening closed.

5 Take a piece of fine string and sew the midpoint of the string in to the V of the heart. Pull the two halves of the string together and tie a loose knot which you pull tight to the V of the heart, leaving the two ends free to tie onto your key.

Left: When you finish the appliqué for a boat it might look a little static. Add life and movement with a running stitch for the sea and the little birds flocking around the mast or swooping down near the deck. Add quilting through the sails and gradually the picture will come to life.

Right: This lampshade and picture were made for a customer with a holiday home by the sea. The boat lampshade suits the lamp base made from an antique spinning bobbin. The trim for the shade is an antique French ticking piped with a vintage ready-made piping in bright red.

Inspired by the seaside

I grew up by the sea, although not the seaside brought to mind by these pictures but the African Atlantic, with beaches of volcanic red sand and rocks coated in smooth black lava. The waves were huge and dangerous and there was no safety in messing about in boats. And yet it has left me with a love of the sea and of boats, whose brightly painted hulls, varnished decks, rigging, and sails offer an endless source of inspiration.

As with all embroidery, you have a better chance of bringing life into your work if you either have, or acquire, a little familiarity with the subject of your embroidery. I have seen boats embroidered with the mast flag flying into the wind! In the little diagram on page 38 you can see the basic parts of a sailing boat. I confess that it is only in writing this book that I have done a little research, rather than relying on vague childhood memories, and so please do not, as I have done in the boat on the lampshade above, attach your mainsail to your tiller!

Boat-and-seagull picture

I used vintage fabrics for this picture, but you could use old shirts or dish towels. My husband has a favorite stripey linen shirt which has now moved to the gardening clothes basket and I am longing for it to fall apart so I can get my hands on the fabric. If you have a nice blue-striped fabric you could use that on one end of the picture: it would make the whole composition a little more interesting. I have included a little seaside patchwork, which you can ignore if you choose. Conversely you could make the whole picture a patchwork and include the larger boat. These boat pictures look charming when displayed in a group. One customer commissioned one for each of her children, with their names on the hulls and their dates of birth on the sails.

Materials

A frame of your choice

A selection of striped and plain fabrics

Threads—If you use strong plain colors for the boat parts—such as the red for the hull of this boat—change the thread in your machine to match.

Bonding web

For the templates for the embroidery see page 136

Stitches used:

Running stitch (see page 128)

Stem stitch (see page 129)

Split stitch (see page 129)

Rollover stitch (see page 131)

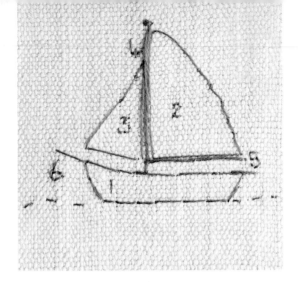

1 Hull **2** Mainsail **3** Jib **4** Mast **5** Boom **6** Bowsprit

4 Decide on the fabrics for your boat parts and fuse these to the bonding web with an iron. Trace the templates for the hull and two sails and transfer these to the paper side of the bonded fabric. Remember to draw the hull and sail going in the opposite direction to that which you want on the picture.

5 Peel off the bonding backing and use tweezers to arrange the boat. When you are satisfied with the arrangement press with an iron. Using a fine machine appliqué stitch, stitch the boat shapes to the base cloth.

Method

1 Cut your base fabric and lay the frame upside down on top of it. Mark the corners of the frame lightly on the base fabric. Your finished work must not stray outside this line.

2 Arrange the fabrics for the little patchwork and pin, baste, and machine stitch them together. You can copy the layout for this project by referring to the detail opposite, but remember to leave enough around the top, left, and bottom edges of the patchwork to fit into the groove at the back of the frame (the rabbet). When you have stitched the patchwork, press the seams open and quilt along the seams with running stitch. Embroider the little gull, starfish, and anchor and any other seaside detail you wish to add (you could use some of the ideas from the nautical laundry bag on pages 40–43).

3 Apply bonding web to the back of the patchwork. Position the patchwork on the base fabric so that the top left corner of the part of the patchwork that will be visible is over the spot you marked in the top left corner in step 1. Iron the reverse of the base fabric to fuse the patchwork to it. Use a machine appliqué stitch to cover the seam of the patchwork and the base fabric.

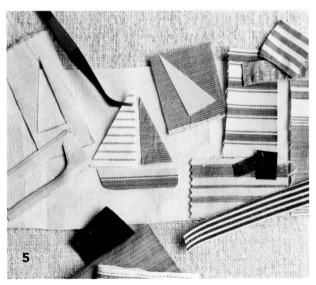

Machine stitching around corners

The trick is to go around curves and corners very slowly and always to lift the foot while the needle is still in the cloth, maneuvering the fabric very slightly with each turn. Personally I prefer always to stitch around a shape clockwise and to think of the stitching coming off the base cloth and catching the edge of the fabric, rather than the other way around. I think this results in a finer stitch.

6 Embroider the detail. It might be helpful here to refer to the diagram of the boat (opposite). In general I think embroidery is more successful if you conjure the thing you are embroidering in your head as you work—both how it looks and how it feels. So if you think about the mast being a pole, it will make sense to work it by doing two rows of very close double thread split stitch and then going over both rows with rollover stitch.

If you imagine how the rigging might attach the mainsail to the boom you can slip the stitch from the sail under the boom embroidery without going through the base cloth, almost as though it really is tied on rather than sewn on. Sometimes I run a curvy wave of very short machine stitches over the sail to give a feeling of movement from the wind. You could also use running stitch on the sails on seen on page 34. If you decide where the rigging is going to be fixed to the mast and again to the hull or boom, you can run a single long stitch between which will give a feeling of tension, which is what you get with real rigging.

7 When you are satisfied with the embroidery, neaten the ends. If you'd like, you can then add little birds to give the piece some movement. However, you must finish each one and neaten them off individually and not carry the thread across because this will show through the fabric.

8 Apply bonding web to the whole of the back of the piece. Peel off and fuse the piece to a piece of lining material. This will make the piece nice and firm for framing and also hide the back of your work.

9 If you are framing the piece yourself work out exactly where to cut the piece down so that it fits neatly into the rabbet at the back of the frame. Clean the glass and place the work face down onto the glass. Then fit the back of the frame, and tape all around the edges. You could use paper tape for this.

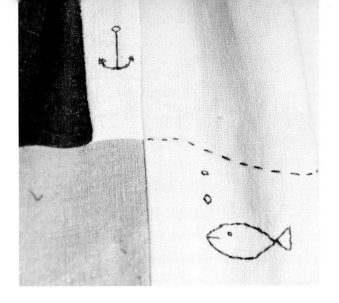

The embroidery in this project is extremely simple. The construction of the bag less so; you will need a sewing machine for it. I have a weakness for anything with a nautical look, and the antique French linens and mattress tickings in soft blue and sandy colors suggest the idea of running stitch waves and sandcastles, seagulls, and little boats. If you'd like, you could also add a favorite line of text about the sea to this. The bag would make a great present for teenagers about to go off to college—they can bring their washing home in it at the end of term.

Nautical laundry bag

Materials

A selection of fabrics with which to make a piece of patchwork with a finished size of 32 inches (length of the bag) x 39 inches (circumference of the bag) plus a seam allowance all around of 1/2 inch. You can of course scale this project down to a much smaller bag.

Plain outer fabric for the bottom of the bag and the band around the top edge of the bag, into which eyelets will be inserted and the cord threaded through. This should be strong fabric but not too thick and cumbersome.

Lining fabric

Threads

Cord for the drawstring

Eyelets and eyelet maker for the drawstring holes

For the templates for the embroidery see page 135

Stitches used:

Running stitch (see page 128)

Straight stitch (see page 128)

Satin stitch (see page 131)

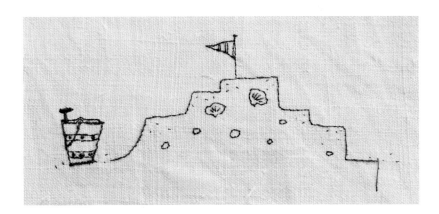

Method

1 First, assemble your pieces of fabric for the patchwork outer layer of the bag. Remember that the pieces at the top of the bag will be drawn together so save the best pieces for what will be the middle and bottom of the bag. Pin, baste, and machine stitch the pieces together until you have a piece of the right size, with a seam allowance all around of ⅜ inch.

2 Decide which sections you are going to embellish with embroidery and how. Sometimes it is a good idea to do one square and then see what that suggests for the next. I use running stitch waves as a connecting thread between the various squares. When you have finished embroidering the panel put the long sides together with right sides together and stitch a seam.

3 Cut a piece of lining fabric the same size as the patchwork and stitch the long sides together with right sides together.

4 Cut outer and lining circles for the bottom of the bag. With right sides together, pin the bottom circle of the bag to the bottom of the patchwork tube so that the pins are spaced at regular intervals and at right angles to the edge. Baste, then machine stitch, feeding the fabric carefully and slowly through the machine as you guide it around the curved edge.

4

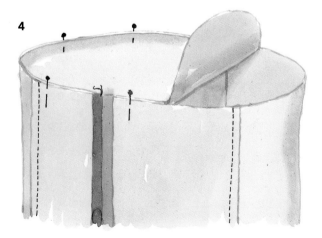

7

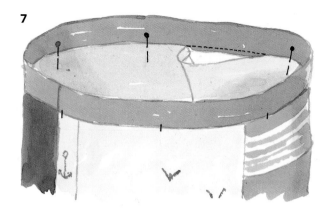

5 Repeat step 4 with the lining tube and circular base, then cut a strip of the plain outer fabric twice the width of the band to go around the top of the bag and stitch the long seam at the side to make a tube.

6 Turn the lining and place it in the bag so that the raw edges are hidden. Baste the lining and the outer part of the patchwork to hold them in place.

7 With right sides together baste and machine stitch the bottom edge of the top band to the top of the bag between the outer fabric and the lining. Turn under the top of the lining and pin in place to cover the seam, thereby joining the top band to the bag.

8 Top stitch around the bag just above the seam between the top of the bag and the band, catching all layers in the line of stitching. Top stitch around the top of the band, about ¼ inch from the top edge.

9 Following the manufacturer's instructions punch eyelet holes at regular intervals around the center of the band for the eyelets. Thread the cord through the eyelets and either tie knots at each end of the cord or tie the ends together.

On the edge

Left and below: I was inspired by the stylized flower on the stamp to use bright colors to decorate the edge of a little vintage hand towel.

Opposite: You could use many of the ideas in this book to add embroidery to the edge of textiles around your home.

Adding decorative details around the home

Adding decoration to the edge of something is one of the simplest forms of embellishment, and embroidering borders along fabric edges is an effective way to introduce embroidery into your home. The decoration can be quite subtle and unexpected: a tiny floral detail at the bottom of a bed skirt or a loose cover, or a grand statement such as a heavily embroidered bed skirt around the frame of a four-poster bed. It is also a good way of using up some of the complicated and highly decorative variations on a stitch, such as the cross pattern using lazy daisy stitch illustrated in the box on page 130. Trails of leaves are one of the most common forms of border decoration, often punctuated with flowers.

The vintage guest towel shown here was embroidered with a tiny floral motif derived from an Indian woodcut stamp. Stamps are very useful for creating the design for a decorative border, particularly if you are not confident about drawing designs yourself. Stamps or woodcuts provide outlines which you can fill with your own colors. It is a good idea to stamp your design on a piece of paper first.

Opposite and left: The edge of the scallop on this cover is the obvious area to embroider, but it would have been just as easy to have done the front edge of the chair pillow, or the two arms. The point is to choose one edge, and keep the decoration simple and subtle.

Below: The craze for redwork led to the introduction of penny squares, little squares of cloth with transferred designs such as this patch of butterflies, which were sold for a penny and used in the making of quilts. These have been widely copied today, as have the red-and-white French redwork trims.

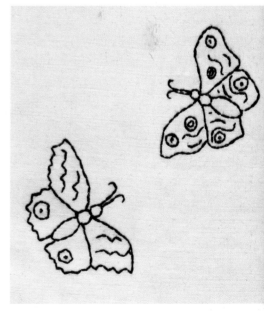

Red stitching on white is known as redwork, and is thought to have started in the mid-nineteenth century in Europe once colorfast red cotton thread had been introduced in Turkey. This innovation meant that the linen and cotton clothes of poor people could be embellished with red cotton embroidery and yet withstand the rough and tumble of washing. As a result redwork became enormously popular. Redwork patterns were printed in magazines and housewives would use them to embellish clothes, tablecloths, and sheets with charming motifs and monograms.

Loose covers for sofas and chairs are a blank canvas for red embroidery. Here a tiny red cross-stitch monogram from an antique French sheet was cut and seamed into the back of the cover, while the front of the chair was embellished with a simple red-and-white tracery of oak leaves, acorns, and flowers, all stitched in stem stitch with a few faux knots to fill the acorns. Try covering up small stains on a loose cover by embroidering a little flower or butterfly over the mark, creating a charming detail that is much nicer to look at.

Slipcovers are an attractive way of adding a bit of softness to the look of plain wooden chairs. You may even want to make a set for special occasions, particularly if you dine in the kitchen but want to create a more formal atmosphere. Or you might wish, as I have done with this project, to create an embellishment for a single chair. I used antique linen, but if you prefer to use a modern fabric, choose one robust enough for regular washing and ironing, and with sufficient weight to hang well. The dropped edge lends itself to some embroidery. Here I chose threads in a gray-green and a blackberry-wine color to work with the antique Swedish desk and chair. You could however embroider the fruits in a raspberry red, and use a brighter green.

Button-on chair cover

Materials

Fabric for cover

Threads

Paper to make a pattern

4 buttons

For the templates for the embroidery and the scallop see page 135

Stitches used:

Slip stitch (see page 133)

Split stitch (see page 129)

Stem stitch (see page 129)

Inspired by antique lace

The embroidery in this design was derived from the pattern in a lace collar belonging to my grandmother. I have simplified it here and there but the central motif of the three fruits is the same. This shows how lace is in fact a form of embroidery and a good source of inspiration for your own designs. You can see further examples of patterns in lace on page 101.

Method

1 Cut a paper pattern to the shape and size of your chair seat. Use the pattern to cut your fabric, adding $^1/_2$ inch seam allowance all round. For the valance, measure around the front and sides of the chair, including the cut-out for the leg. Add $^1/_2$ inch seam allowance all round and and $1^3/_4$ inches for the buttonhole overlap. For the depth allow $2^3/_4$ inches to the narrowest part of the scalloped edge. Create paper patterns using the scallop template. Repeat to make a pattern for the back valance, and then cut both pieces out in fabric.

1

2

2 Iron the lower edge of the scallop, and cut a small notch into the scallop. Turn under the hem on the scalloped edge twice, baste, and slip stitch the hem.

3 Pin, baste, and machine stitch the valance pieces to the seat piece, right sides together. Turn under twice and slip stitch the remaining hems. The back panel is embroidered in double thread and I have filled the leaves with single-thread split stitch. On the side panels I varied things by using single thread stem stitch and no fills.

4 Place the cover on the chair and mark the buttons and buttonholes. Make two buttonholes on each of the overlaps and sew the buttons in place.

4

Making paper templates

When you are fitting an embroidery to something which requires a degree of precision in the layout, it is useful to make paper templates and draw the design in full to make sure that it fits. Unlike something like the bookend on pages 28–31, which is something I stitched without any form of preliminary sketch, I drew the design for this project in full and then lightly transferred it to the linen using a very soft pencil tracing. You cannot afford to find that you have reached the corner and run out of space for the design!

Antique decorative edging

Browsing through vintage textiles stalls at brocantes or vide-greniers in France you will often find lengths of scallop-edged trims, embroidered with red stem and satin stitching depicting fruit, vegetables, ceramics, and other household objects. These redwork trims were embroidered by French women during the first half of the nineteenth century. One reason the borders were so popular might be explained by the rather grim kitchens. Everything was dark and undecorated, and these bright strips of embroidery were not only a matter of pride, showing the skill of the housewife, but a way of introducing some color and cheer.

Opposite: An antique country cupboard is used to store kitchen china. The deep shelves are edged with a red trim that was worked by a French housewife in the middle of the nineteenth century.

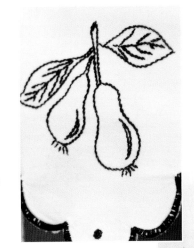

Left: These pears were almost certainly not done using a transfer. I love the little stitches for the sometimes quite prickly hairs at the base of the pear, a detail from someone who handled pears, and who probably cooked up a great *tarte aux poires.*

Right: The coffee pot may have belonged to the housewife who stitched this trim. It has some Eastern influence, as did so many of the French ceramics of the time.

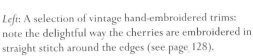

Left: A selection of vintage hand-embroidered trims: note the delightful way the cherries are embroidered in straight stitch around the edges (see page 128).

Occasionally it can be hard to identify a particular object that has been embroidered, and this is probably because it is a depiction of something hand-made by the man of the house. Not all of the trims were used for kitchen shelves: the deeper ones were used to decorate the chimneypiece over the cooking range and these often have stains from bearing witness to the odd splash of sauce from the kitchen pot.

Embroidered shelf trims can also create a charming effect in antique armoires where linen or china is stored. In a linen closet you could stitch the name of the items stored on that shelf—sheets, pillowcases, blankets, and so on.

I felt inspired to create a length of shelf edging for this beach house kitchen with its collection of quirky ceramics and bottles. The cupboard in a family kitchen is full of memories, and so I followed the French tradition of embroidering a collection of favorite things: little bottles filled with flowers, tureens, chocolate pots, and old stone jars. If you don't want to make a shelf trim, you may want to adopt this idea for the bottom of a kitchen shade. I happened to have a long piece of scalloped edging from the bottom of an old bedspread. I tried to give the piece a more contemporary feel by working it in a single mid-blue thread. You could personalize it by adding family members' names on plates or jars.

Kitchen shelf edging

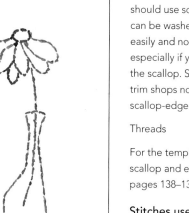

Materials

A piece of fabric long enough for the shelf plus a ³/₄ inch turn allowance. For this project you should use something that can be washed and ironed easily and not too thick, especially if you have to make the scallop. Some ribbon and trim shops now sell suitable scallop-edged trims.

Threads

For the templates for the scallop and embroidery see pages 138–139

Stitches used:

Blanket stitch (see page 129)

Stem stitch (see page 129)

Method

1 Using the scallop template cut the bottom edge. Hem the edges following the instructions for the chair cover on page 53. If you would like to embroider the scalloped edge use a fine blanket stitch worked in double thread (single is finer but will take a very long time).

2 For the embroidery, start in the center and work to the sides; you will achieve a better balance. If you trace the design from the template, then start the tracing in the center as well.

3 It is important to keep the back very tidy, and to sew in your ends neatly, as any kitchen textile has to withstand regular washing. If you decide to make this using red thread, remember that most modern red threads tend to bleed slightly, especially if you wet them when threading the needle. (Using a needle threader helps avoid this problem.) Fix the trim in place on the shelf with tiny tacks at each end and perhaps one in the center if it is very wide.

This headboard was made from an old tongue-and-grooved panel, some antique brackets, and a shelf, its edge now softened with a cover. If you don't want to make a headboard cover, this design could just as easily be used to decorate the edge of a table cloth, or a window pelmet. I used appliqué to create the substance of the design. For the trees I used linen which I painted with very diluted watercolor paints, and I think this lends a painterly quality to the piece. I discovered that linen holds watercolor paint well when I had a mishap with a cup of coffee just as I finished stitching another embroidery. Nothing would get rid of the stain completely so I decided to have a go at camouflaging it with paint.

Headboard shelf cover

Materials

Linen for the base fabric

Assorted fabric scraps in different colors and patterns for the appliqué elements

Bonding web

Threads

For the templates for the scallop and embroidery see pages 136–137

Stitches used:

Stab stitch (see page 133)

Straight stitch (see page 128)

Knot stitch (see page 131)

Method

1 Measure the edge to which you plan to fix the finished piece. Allow about eight inches at either end to wrap around the sides. Cut out the scallops and then hem around all edges following the instructions for the chair cover on page 53.

2 Fuse your chosen fabrics for the appliqué with bonding web and trace the designs onto the paper side. Remember that when you want something to point left you must draw it pointing right on the paper.

3 Position the elements for the design on the base fabric. Peel off the bonding web and fuse the designs. Sew the designs to the cover using a fine machine appliqué stitch (see page 133) with the threads matching the colors of the fabrics as closely as possible. Some of the pieces are very small and a good trick is to machine stitch very slowly. On something like the tiny scalloped window awnings I sometimes turn the wheel of the machine by hand to have increased control.

3

4 Some of the tinier pieces can be applied with short stab stitches. In this piece the red flower petals are made from a tiny piece of Victorian fabric that is too delicate to withstand machine appliqué.

4

5 Now add the hand-embroidered details, all of which are worked in a combination of short and long straight stitches and knot stitch. The tree branches are worked in two strands, but everything else is single strand.

Remember that, as with all the projects in the book, this is just a starting point for your own creativity. So if you want to add more flowers, or work the trees in the same way as the tree in the bookend project on pages 28–31, then feel free to do so.

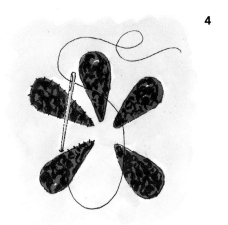

Painting linen with watercolor paint

Choose a fairly stiff but textured linen—anything too fine does not absorb color evenly. Place the linen on a piece of plastic or a flattened polyethylene bag. Dip your brush in the solid color and rinse the brush into a small jar of water. Keep adding solid color until you think you have the right shade. I use a china plate or bowl to mix the color so I can see what it will look like on the white fabric. Remember that natural greens have more yellow than blue. Test the color on a piece of card paper and when you think you have the color you want, apply the dilute color very slowly to the linen. Allow each droplet to be absorbed by the cloth and then quickly add the next brushful.

Hang the cloth to dry, then iron, and review it. You may have to add another layer of color. You can add a different color—for example a soft blue—when the first color is completely dry. Just remember to add the second color a fraction of an inch away from the first to avoid too much overlap.

Above and right: Watercolor inks are good for painting fabrics as long as you dilute them. There is no hard-and-fast recipe, but err on the side of extremely dilute and add color very gradually. There are many precedents for combining painted fabric with embroidery, notably in woolwork pictures worked on painted silk backgrounds. I have mostly used this technique for framed pictures, and the color does not fade. I do not suggest using it on projects that will get a lot of wear. For those, you could try hand-dyeing in the microwave. If something must be cleaned, I suggest dry-cleaning only.

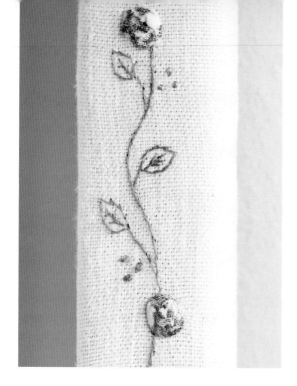

In the hallway of Monk's House in Sussex, England, the former home of Virginia Woolf where we lived for just over a decade, there was a tapestry mirror frame which was one of the writer's favorite possessions, and it gave me the idea to use embroidery for covering a small mirror frame. You could use any number of the ideas in this book to decorate a mirror frame, but this little frame suggested a trail of roses. If you want to make something more dramatic you can cover a larger and wider frame with the poppies from the director's chair covers on pages 94–97.

Rosebud mirror frame

Materials

A frame—for this project you want a small frame that is no more than 2 inches wide

Light wadding

A staple gun and staples

Base fabric—something with a reasonably strong weave

Printed lawn, silk, or other lightweight material for the roses

Threads

For the template for the embroidery see page 135

Stitches used:

Stem stitch (see page 129)

Stab stitch (see page 133)

Method

1 Cut two strips for the top and bottom and two for the sides in both the light wadding and the base fabric. Allow enough fabric on either side to fold around the frame and into the rabbet. You can always trim extra fabric off but it becomes a very fiddly job if you leave yourself short of fabric.

2 Make the mitered seams in the wadding, then trim and lay the wadding over the frame, folding it onto the back outside edge, and affixing it with staples. Pull the wadding around the frame and into the rabbet, again securing with staples. Trim off any excess.

3 Make a template for the long and short sides of the frame, ending where the corners join. Lay this on top of your base fabric and mark the corners lightly to demarcate the area which you are going to decorate. Make sure you keep the grain of the linen straight. Lightly trace your design onto the cloth. The design does not have to be exactly symmetrical but the top and bottom and two sides must balance each other. You can shorten or extend the repeat pattern to fit your chosen frame.

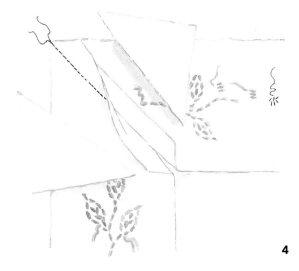

4

4 The leaves and stems are worked in single thread stem stich, the dots in double thread. Add the roses (see box opposite) and iron. Seam the four pieces together at the corners, iron, and trim the seams.

5 Fold the inner corners into the rabbet of the frame and, making sure it is all going to fit, staple each corner in place, this time working from the inside to the outside. Work around the frame, fixing the fabric in place over the wadding with a staple gun and taking care not to pull it so tight that the grain is not straight. Fix the mirror glass and backing in place and tape around the edges to finish.

Fashioning fabric roses

For the roses you need very soft, lightweight material that folds easily and does not create too much bulk. For years I had some exquisite antique French silk from a damaged scarf, and now I am working my way through the skirt made from antique lawn printed with little roses. You might find that dress fabric is better for this. The finished roses are about $1/4$ inch in diameter, for which you need to cut a piece about $3/4$ x $1/2$ inch.

First fold the edge furthest away from you over and pleat the piece of fabric between the thumb and forefinger. Fix this pleat with a couple of stitches and then sew it to the cloth where you want the rose to be (1). Now you simply continue pleating and manipulating the fabric working in a counterclockwise spiral, stitching the pleats down with the tiniest stab stitches, tucking any stray ends under as you work (2). You can use this technique on pillows which are not going to get a lot of wear, or make a basket of roses instead of the daisy basket on pages 24–27, like the one shown below.

1

2

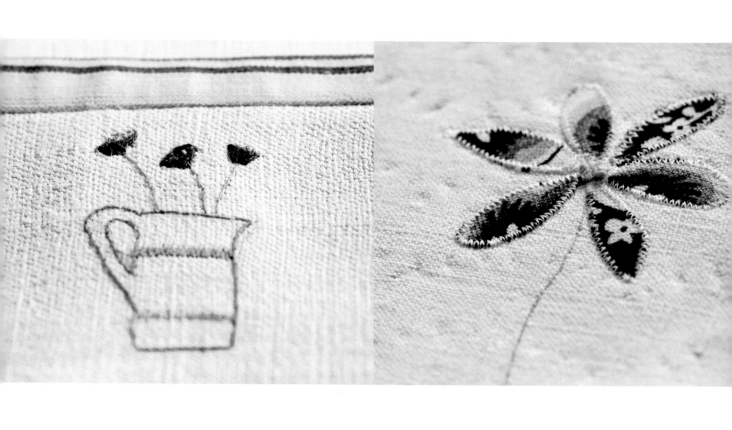

At the table

The importance of table settings

Taking a cloth from the linen closet, starched and ironed, and casting it over the table, has been the preamble to special family occasions for centuries. Nowadays rustic chic permits us to eschew any form of fabric table covering for everyday family meals. Never underestimate though the emotional association of the tablecloth. My mother took her best damask cloth to every country we lived in, using it for dinner parties and Christmas, and today it has acquired a luxurious sheen from half a century of hot washes, starchings, and ironings, and I think of family Christmas meals every time I see it folded in her linen closet.

Creating cloths or runners for the family table is a particularly significant way of introducing embroidery to the home. Just make

Inspiration from heirlooms

An article in The Huffington Post *described a family heirloom tablecloth that had been made by asking successive guests to write or draw on the cloth in fabric marker pen, over which the hostess embroidered after each event, thus creating a permanent record of all her dinner parties and family gatherings.*

Far left: If you are lucky enough to have inherited piles of linen from relatives, take a closer look at them for inspiration for your embroidery projects. For example, this starch white tablecloth inspired the idea of using a one color design, which gives it a contemporary look.

Left: The dots diminishing in size around a circle between the groups of flowers on this cloth is a lovely idea.

sure you choose a good quality base cloth that will stand up to years of washing, and use colorfast thread. I have taken to soaking my red thread bundles in a bowl of very hot water to allow any residual color to bleed out. There is nothing more upsetting than having a supposedly colorfast thread bleed into the surrounding fabric, either through handling or the first wash, and reds are notoriously badly behaved.

Placemats can be a charming way of decorating the family table for everyday meals. Make a different mat for each member of the family using similar colors and fabrics. Or take the patterns on your china as a starting point: vintage ceramics often have beautiful flower or fruit shapes which translate well into appliqué and embroidery.

Below: The embroidery on the placemat has been positioned so it can be seen by the diner. The little pot of red flowers picks up the embroidery motif.

This project may be worked in either simple back stitch or stem stitch and so while there is a considerable amount of embroidery, it is good for people who have not embroidered before. A few years ago I could not resist a set of three vintage French roller towels and finally found a use for one of them with this project. The towel was the perfect width for a table runner and there was no need to hem the sides. I think it works best if the finished runner is slightly longer than the table. You could also embroider this design around the edge or down the middle of a tablecloth.

Pinwheel table runner

Materials

A piece of fabric at least as long as your table plus an allowance for the hem. If you can find a slightly heavier linen it will be easier to work. Ideally it should have a bit of texture.

Threads

Plain red fabric—I have used vintage fabric to create the solid flower petals, but you could fill these in with satin or darning stitch if you prefer

Mother of pearl or shirt buttons

Bonding web

Muslin cloth

For the template for the embroidery see page 139

Stitches used:

Stem stitch (see page 129)

Back stitch (see page 128)

Knot stitch (see page 131)

Satin stitch (see page 131)

Method

1 First, hem all the edges. You can do this by machine if you prefer but I think a hand-stitched hem gives a gentler finish, as do properly mitered corners.

2 I did not use a tracing or pattern for the embroidery: I simply took up my needle and thread and slowly sketched the first trail, and then imitated this with varying degrees of success along the edges of the runner. If you prefer, you can use the template to create a tracing. First enlarge it to the size that you want.

3 Transfer the template to your base cloth. In order to keep your trail aligned along the edge of the runner, position a flower or leaf near the edge and ensure that in each pattern repeat the flower or leaf is the same distance from the edge.

4 Embroider the design using stem stitch or back stitch. The effect is nicer with stem stitch, particularly when going around curves. However, you also get an interesting effect if you do simple back stitch but instead of going into the same hole as the stitch behind you, split the base of the stitch with your needle.

5 For the solid flower petals fuse bonding web to the wrong side of a small piece of fabric. Now draw the petal shapes on the paper side and cut them out. Peel off the paper and position them. I find a pair of craft tweezers useful for this. Fuse them to the runner using an iron. I always use a muslin cloth between the work and the iron at this stage.

6 Using a sewing machine appliqué the petals to the runner. You can stitch them on by hand but they will be more robust if done by machine. The trick with the curves is to go very slowly and stop to turn the fabric with the machine needle down. Pull the threads through to the wrong side and tie or stitch them down. I had not planned to use solid flowers when I started

but felt the design needed more impact. If you did not want to make solid flowers, it might look interesting to embroider larger flowers like these in outline, employing the same back stitch, perhaps with an extra thread for emphasis. For most of the design I used three threads. The little dots are worked in simple satin stitch, and the filling for the leaves was made with knot stitch.

7 Add buttons to the center of each of the solid petalled flowers. You could choose red ones to match the petals but I preferred the subtler tone of the mother-of-pearl.

Inset opposite: Rather than having perfectly matching napkins I like to follow the theme of the runner and embroider different elements onto each napkin. This allows me to play around with design ideas.

The construction of the placemats in this section is the same; the decoration of the top surface varies. I think it is more fun to make variations rather than make them all the same. Choose a couple contrasting fabrics and arrange them differently—a band down the side of one, a scalloped band along the bottom of another, a band across the top of another, each decorated differently. For a family you could personalize each placemat and napkin ring with initials. You could also make little patches of embroidery, like these daisies worked in a simple back stitch.

Placemats

Materials

Two contrasting fabrics, one of which will also edge the placemat

Interlining

Lining for the reverse

Small scraps of floral or plain cream linen for the flower petals

Bonding web

Threads

Buttons (optional)

Note

All the fabrics should be robust, colorfast, and washable.

For the template for the embroidery see page 140

Stitches used:

Back stitch (see page 128)

Chain stitch (see page 130)

Stem stitch (see page 129)

Knot stitch (see page 131)

Satin stitch (see page 131)

Slip stitch (see page 133)

Method

1 Wash the interlining in the hottest wash recommended to pre-shrink it.

2 Measure the size of placemat you would like to have. Check the size of the plates you will be using, and make sure there is room for a glass and some cutlery to the side of the plate. Cut a piece of plain linen, a piece of pre-shrunk interlining, and the lining (for the back) to this size plus $^1/_2$ inch all around seam allowance.

3 Put the interlining and lining to one side. Now decorate your front piece. For the design on the previous pages I incorporated the stripe within the fabric, adding appliquéd flowers on one side. To make the flowers, fuse bonding web to the reverse of the fabric and use the petal template to create flower petals and leaves. Use a craft tweezers to place them carefully and then press and stitch them to the placemat using machine appliqué. The stem on the flowers placemat is worked in chain stitch using three strands. The embroidered patch of linen is applied in the same way, and finished with a small button on one corner.

4 To make the scalloped green band for the placemat shown opposite, fuse bonding web to a piece of plain green fabric about a third as deep as the overall depth of the placemat. Using the scallop template draw a scalloped edge along the top edge of the bonding web paper. Cut along this scalloped edge. Now peel off the bonding web paper and position the green fabric strip on the bottom edge of the plain linen piece and iron to fuse. Fix with a machine appliqué stitch.

5 Apply the floral-patterned petals for the flowers as in step 3. The embroidered flowers with the dot-filled petals are worked in two strands, using stem stitch for the outline, knot stitch for the petal fill, and satin stitch for the centers. The smaller flowers are all worked in satin stitch.

Making up the placemats

1 Pin the front piece to the interlining and lining piece. Cut four lengths of the edging fabric $^1/_2$ inch longer than the sides. With right sides together, stitch these to the sides of the placemats, stopping about $^3/_8$ inch before each corner.

1

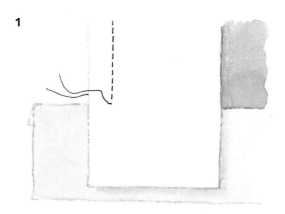

2 Where the edging fabric pieces meet at the corners, cut the edges on the diagonal and stitch them together to make neat mitered seams.

3 Turn in $^1/_4$ inch all around the edging strip, clipping the corners where the edges overlap, and press. Fold over each mitered corner, and then turn in the edging strip all the way around the mat, mitering the corners as you fold. Pin in place. Hem all around using slip stitch, including the folded miters. Iron to finish.

3

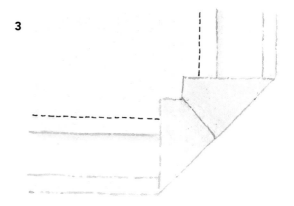

Below: Tiny scraps of fabric left over from kitchen curtains were used to make the flower petals on this placemat. The little basket on the napkin ring was made using appliqué, while the flowers are simply small short stitches layered on top of each other.

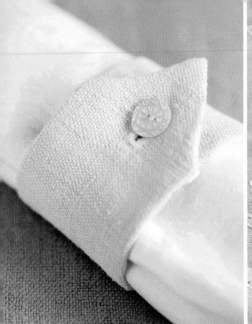

Napkin rings

These are based on the napkin rings we had to make at school. I added bonding web to make them stiffer, but you could leave this out if you prefer. You could use a snap to fasten them or a button with a thread loop if the idea of making a buttonhole appalls. If the top fabric is not too thin you could use a colored lining, but don't choose unwieldy fabrics as the hem needs to be very small and neat. A set of these would make a charming wedding gift.

Materials

Fabric for the top and lining

Threads

Snap or button for fastening

Bonding web (optional)

For the templates for the napkin ring and embroidery see page 140

Stitches used:

A variety of stitches, depending on design chosen

Slip stitch (see page 133)

Method

1 Using the template cut the top and lining fabrics. Press a $1/4$ inch hem all around the top fabric. Embroider either the designs shown above, or your own, or use ideas from elsewhere in the book. Keep the reverse of the work as neat as you can, trimming loose threads.

2 Fuse bonding web (if using) to the wrong side of the lining fabric. Peel off and lay the lining, right side up, inside the embroidered linen. Pushing the folded edge out of the way, press. Then re-press the folded edge and turn it under. Slip stitch the hem to the lining. Make a buttonhole and sew on the button or add the snap.

Egg cozy

Materials

Scraps of old blanket or felted wool

Silk threads and yarn of your choice

Bonding web

For the templates for the cozy and embroidery see page 140

Stitches used:

Satin stitch (see page 131)

Straight stitch (see page 128)

Stem stitch (see page 129)

Blanket stitch (see page 129)

Method

1 Using the templates cut two pieces of your fabric and the flower and scallop. Attach the flower and scallop to the front of the egg cozy with bonding web and satin stitch. Add embroidered flowers and leaves using straight stitch and stem stitch.

2 Pin and stitch together using blanket stitch and yarn. Finish with blanket stitch around the bottom edge.

The soft stuff

Introducing texture and pattern

Embroidered pillows and throws are a simple way to add beauty and comfort to your home. Remember though that less is more: a host of little pillows scattered about for decorative effect may look fine on a sofa in a hotel lobby but at home is plain annoying. Sofas nowadays are big so make sure your pillows are in proportion, large enough to sink into, and provide support; it is very easy to have feather pads made up in exactly the size you want. If you want a pillow to sink into on your large sofa, make it a large one with a proper feather pad in a comfortable fabric. Don't embroider a pillow for the large comfortable sofa and then scream every time someone leans against it. Make sure your embroidery is sufficiently robust or position it on the cushion so that it does not get so much wear, as in the Harebells cushion project on page 88. The same applies to throws: decide whether your throw is there to disguise the sofa or keep you warm. If the former, embroider the part of the throw that lies along the top of the sofa.

Think about a variety of textures. Vintage blankets make wonderfully cozy throws or pillows. You could cut them up, dye them different colors in the washing machine, and stitch patches together using blanket stitch, perhaps decorating some of the patches with embroidered flowers.

But remember that too many pillows can be a cause of marital disharmony, especially on the bed.

Above: One of the pleasures of using appliqué is that you can extract painterly colors from small areas of patterned fabric. The restrained taupey gray and washed-lemon linen used for this pillow were snipped out of a piece of antique fabric with the colors of a Matisse painting.

Opposite: In this elegantly spare room the subtle colors of the patterned antique linens have been echoed in the embroidered pillows, adding a layer of texture and detail without being too obtrusive.

Now that we mostly use comforters on our beds, I think a number of us have beautiful blankets packed away in linen closets. But the quality of these wool blankets can make them wonderful pillowcases. You can dye them successfully in your machine, just remember not to use a very hot wash or they will felt. While it would be possible to make a pillowcase with felted wools, it would not be as cozy.

Daisy blanket pillowcase

Materials

Old woolen blankets in contrasting colors

Dye (optional)

Pillow pad—Try to use feather pads where you can for pillows (unless you cannot for health reasons) as they make pillows so much softer and look more luxurious.

Threads

For the template for the embroidery see page 140

Stitches used:

Lazy daisy stitch (see page 130)

Stem stitch (see page 129)

Blanket stitch (see page 129)

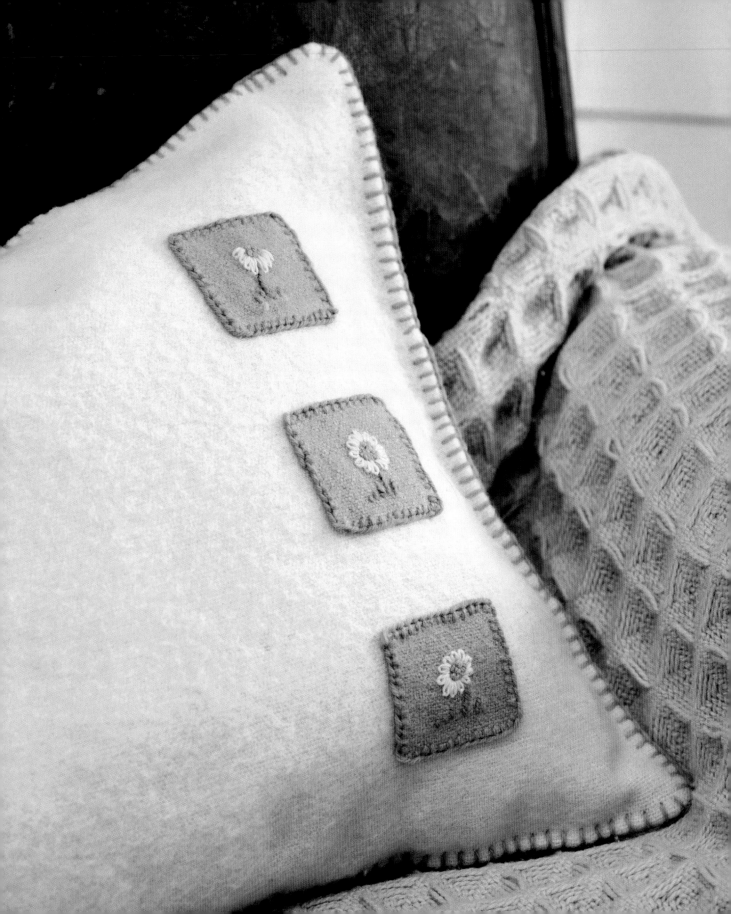

Method

1 Decide on the size of your pillow. Cut the front and two pieces for the back large enough to overlap to form the opening. If your blanket has a blanket-stitched edge you can use this for the top half of the back.

2 Cut three little patches from a contrasting blanket. I have used a dyed blanket here for the contrasting patches. It is very straightforward to dye small pieces of fabric in the microwave—simply follow the dye manufacturer's instructions.

3 Embroider a daisy on each patch. These daisies are worked in lazy daisy stitch and stem stitch. Start your daisy with the middle petal and work out from there, and always add the stems at the end.

4 Pin the patches to the front of the pillow and baste. Stitch them to the front of the pillow using small, close blanket stitches. Pin the front and backs right sides together. Don't forget the backs of the pillow overlap, so for a short stretch you will be attaching three layers of fabric together. Stitch the pillow together. Turn and press.

5 Pinching the seam together, stitch all around the pillow using a larger, more widely spaced blanket stitch than for the patches.

Decorating traditional wool blankets

One of the most charming embroidered blankets I have seen was a plain cream one with the words "Oh, to be in England now that April's there" embroidered in large looped writing across the top. If you're not ready to put words on your blanket, you can have stripes running across the top end, and you can decorate these with running stitches of different colors, or outlines of flowers and leaves.

One of the most beautiful fabrics to have passed through my workroom was a piece of vintage linen containing a myriad of colors reminding me of Monet's great garden at Giverny. Having made it into pillows I was left with a few scraps and was struck by the pale lemon yellow, pinky beige, and soft ointment pink which I have used to create the appliqué for the flowers in this pillow, adding dotty flowers in lilac between. The pillow adds subtle texture to a group of plainer pillows. Arranging the panel of embroidery at the top of the pillow lends it a contemporary feel, and means that the area with the embroidery does not get as much wear. This is a good way to use up scraps of fabric you may have used in decorating schemes.

Harebells pillow

Materials

Printed material scraps for the appliqué—I have used vintage fabric but you can see from the colors the palette if you want to achieve a close copy.

Card to make templates of harebells and daisy flowers.

Bonding web

Threads

Base fabric for the pillow

Button (optional)

For the template for the embroidery see page 141

Stitches used:

Stem stitch (see page 129)

Satin stitch (see page 131)

Method

1 Decide on the size of your pillow. The one in this photograph was $17\frac{1}{2}$ inch wide.

2 Cut the panel for the embroidery, slightly less than a third of the pillow front, but remember to add $\frac{1}{2}$ inch seam allowance.

3 Fuse bonding web to the reverse of your printed fabric. Make card templates for the petals and flowers.

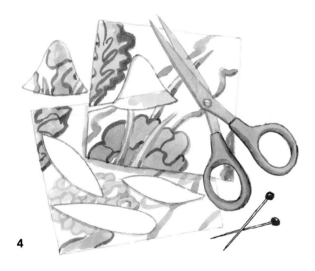

4

4 Lay these on the paper side of the bonding web fabric and draw around them, making sure that on the fabric side you have captured the colors that you want. You might feel confident enough to cut the petals and flowers out freehand without a template, but make sure you have fused the bonding web to the fabric first.

5 Use craft tweezers to place the flowers. Don't make them all the same: have your harebells blowing this way or that way. Peel off the bonding web and press. Secure to the fabric with a delicate machine appliqué.

6 Use single thread stem stitch to create the stems and the blades of grass, and satin stitch for the lilac dots. The elongated stems give the design a more stylized, contemporary feel.

7 Sew the panels for the front together and sew the front of the pillow to the back, using the fastening of your choice. I used a zipper, but you could use two back pieces with a deep overlap, or buttons.

It is a good idea when starting an embroidered piece to gather things together to make a color palette. It doesn't matter if you don't use everything in the embroidery—the idea is to experiment with mixing the colors. It took me quite a while to decide on the right "tender" green for this project and it helped to have all the colors together to play with. This pillow measures 20 x 12 inches, with the central panel being 7$\frac{1}{2}$ inches wide. It is a good size for a small formal chair. This is my first attempt at traditional embroidery and I have no doubt that there are many readers who can improve upon it.

Violet pillow

Materials

Enough linen for the central panel, and contrasting linen for the side panels and back

Lining fabric

Threads

Edging tape (optional)

Button (optional)

For the template for the embroidery see page 142

Stitches used:

Satin stitch (see page131)

Stem stitch (see page 129)

Method

1 Cut the three panels for the front of the pillow and stitch together. Transfer the design to the central panel.

2 Use a combination of satin and stem stitch to complete the embroidery.

3 Do not be afraid to change or add details: so, for example, you could add a butterfly from the panel on pages 120–23, or have little bees like those on pages 58–61. Neaten and sew in any loose ends.

4 Sew the edging strips on alongside the panel, if you are using them, then make up the pillow. If you decide to use a button fastening it would make a lovely touch to embroider some tiny violets and cover the buttons with them (see page 119).

Using openwork hems

Whenever I use the embroidery from vintage cloths I always keep the openwork hems because they are very useful for framing embroidered panels on pillows (see above). For this project I used some which happened to be a similar color to the vintage hand-dyed sheet I used for the body of the pillow.

I like to use director's chairs as dining chairs. They are comfortable and offer great scope for decoration. You can paint them and have the slings remade in antique linen, with a simple detail such as the chair on page 6, or make the chairs a key feature of your decorating scheme by combining embroidery with a contrasting textile, such as the chairs in this project. I think that unless you are a trained upholsterer it is always worth paying a professional to put it all together for you using reinforcing interlining and strong stitching. If you want to have a go yourself you can follow the instructions overleaf. It is nice to decorate both sides of the chairs as we have done here, but using the contrasting fabric differently on each side. As with all the projects, feel free to adapt the recipe. You do not have to use a contrasting fabric but could have the whole sling in plain linen. Use designs from other projects in the book, or these flowers in different colors.

Director's chair cover

Materials

A director's chair

Strong plain linen, vintage if possible as the weave is strong

Contrasting fabric—I used ticking

Plain linen for lining

Wadding $1/8$ inch thick

Threads

For the template for the embroidery see pages 140–141

Stitches used:

Satin stitch (see page 131)

Stem stitch (see page 129)

Split stitch (see page 129)

Left and below: These flowers are like the squiggly flowers that children draw and are easy to stitch freehand. You can follow the template exactly or add in touches of your own. The poppies work well stitched in single thread, while the squiggly flowers are best in double thread.

Method

1 Take your measurements from your chair. The best way to make sure your fabric is exactly the right size is to unpick the existing sling and use it as a template. Allow plenty of room around it for the seams. Cut a piece of fabric for the front and back of the sling, and then a piece of wadding small enough to sit just inside the seam line. I created two different sized panels for the embroidery, with ticking panels along the top of one and set on each side of the other.

2 Decide how big you want your embroidered panel to be and cut it from the linen fabric. Mark the middle of the panel and work from the center outwards. If you do not feel confident working freehand, then lightly trace the templates onto the linen. The flowers were worked in satin stitch and the stems and leaves in stem stitch. Cut sections of ticking to the right size to create pieces the same size as your back and front pieces, allowing an extra $1/2$ inch for seams. Place right sides together with the embroidered panels, then machine stitch in place. Open out the seams and iron them flat.

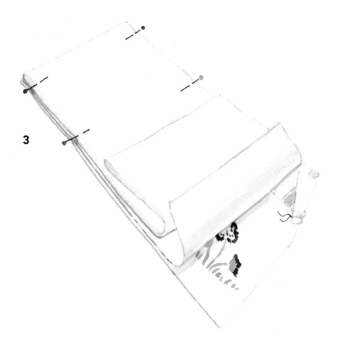

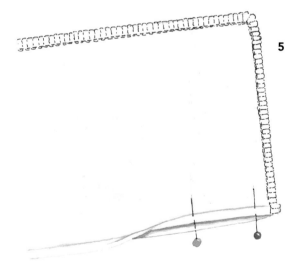

3 Pin the front embroidered panel to the plain linen piece, with the wadding on top. Machine stitch around the sides and top, making sure you don't stitch through the wadding as this will create a ridge when you turn the sling the right way out.

4 Lay the embroidered back panel over the front section, rights sides together, and the second plain linen piece over the top. Pin and machine stitch around the two sides and top edge through all five layers. Finish the raw edges with overlock stitch to strengthen them.

5 To finish the bottom edge, turn under twice and pin and baste in place. Turn out to the right way, then machine stitch all around the bottom edge.

The inspiration for this headboard cover was twofold: first, a stenciled flour sack dating from 1860, with leaves, stems, and little fruits. Second, the leaves on the exquisitely worked antique French linen sheet used on the same bed in a spare room. You could work all of the leaves with a variety of embroidered fillings—knot stitch, satin stitch, darning stitch, and so on. However, I thought it would be fun to create a variety of textures by using different laces, openwork, and whitework to create the leaves and birds, stitching around the edges either by hand or using machine appliqué. This design was worked on a French antique linen sheet which has been dyed.

Appliquéd headboard cover

Materials

A piece of fabric 2 inches larger all round than the headboard you are going to cover. It might also be possible to make a fitted slipcover but we simply stapled the fabric to the rear of the headboard. If you prefer you could also get an upholsterer to do this for you, or ask someone to make up the slipcover once you have done the hard bit!

A selection of fabrics for the leaves, stems, and birds

Threads

Bonding web

For the template for the embroidery see page 141

Stitches used:

Satin stitch (see page 131)

Split stitch (see page 129)

Knot stitch (see page 131)

Method

1 Decide where you want to position the design. This one was put into the top 8 inches of a standard single bed headboard. Mark the center point. You can use the templates supplied, but you might prefer to draw the leaves and the stems freehand. The effect will be looser and have more movement than if you make it entirely symmetrical with all the leaves the same size.

2 Fuse all the fabrics you plan to use for the birds, leaves, and stems to bonding web. Draw a selection of leaves on the papery side and cut them out. I find it helpful to use very sharp small scissors for this. Draw and cut out the stems in the same way and position these first. Peel off the papery backing and fuse the stems to the base fabric.

3 Using craft tweezers, position the leaves and flowers along the stems, using different laces and textures for each section of stem. It is helpful if you place a ruler or piece of thread across the base fabric while you do this so that you remain roughly on a straight line. Fuse the branches and leaves to the base. Machine appliqué them to the base fabric. Then position the birds, and then their wings and attach them in the same way.

Finding antique lace

At almost every flea market there are dealers with a scrap bag of lace odds and ends. Look through these carefully because even if the pieces are torn and tatty there may be treasure in the patterns which can be adapted for embroidering. Notice the lilies, roses, snowflakes, and crowns in these pieces of lace.

4 Once the leaves and birds are stitched down, add the dots in satin stitch in between the leaves and branches. Stitch the legs, eyes, and markings onto the birds using split stitch and satin stitch, and then add dots formed from knot stitch to some of the leaves. The stitched detail here is one idea only. You can try out variations; perhaps lines to replicate the veins in leaves, or stitch around the outside of each leaf. You could even work the entire design in colored fabrics on cream linen. Embroidering a design should be like following a recipe—have the courage to throw in your own ingredients.

Embroidering an entire quilt would probably be beyond the patience and available time of most people. I admired this quilt made by my mother-in-law, who has stitched and quilted with the same circle of friends for more than twenty years. The idea is so clever; she has used tiny scraps of vintage embroidery as the centerpiece of each section of log cabin piecing, the latter all in white and ivory antique linens. The main thing is that the overall color is white, with tiny jewel-like windowpanes of color. Of course you could also embroider the central squares yourself, using ideas from elsewhere in the book.

Log cabin quilt with vintage embroidery

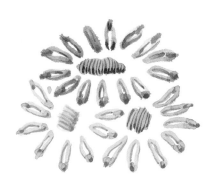

Materials

A selection of white and off-white linens and cottons for the surrounding strips

Embroidered patches for the central squares

Ruler, card, and pencil

Interlining

Lining fabric

Edging fabric

Thread

Stitches used:

A variety of stitches if you choose to embroider your own central panels

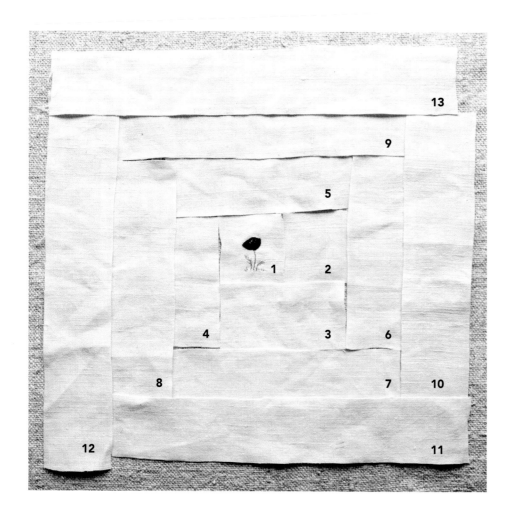

Method

1 First decide on the size of your finished quilt and calculate how many log cabin squares you will need. It is best to have an odd number for aesthetic balance. So for example, if your bed is 4 ½ feet wide and each finished log cabin section is 13 inches plus seam allowance, you would need five sections across. The sizes of each finished square of log cabin depends on the size of your embroidered squares. It is best to make the individual sections first and then have fun working out how to join them together.

2 Select patches to embroider, iron them, and cut to squares of the same size. One way to continue is to make yourself card templates for the different numbered strips and then allocate certain fabric to each numbered strip of the log cabin pattern, and cut all of them out at once. This will have the effect of creating a pattern of the different shades of whites across the quilt.

3 Sew the log cabin squares. Always start with the center square and add the next strip in the order shown in the photograph, working in a clockwise direction around the square. When you have enough squares, iron all the seams open flat and lay them out as you prefer. Stitch all the squares together to form the top layer.

4 Cut a piece of interlining the size of the finished quilt and pin it to the wrong side of the log cabin fronts. Quilting at this stage is optional. However yu may want to quilt the side of the seam lines, which will add texture and strength to the quilt.

5 Cut the lining. Pin the wrong side to the interlining. If you have not quilted the top baste across the quilt in a cross shape to make sure it is all lined up. Iron.

6 Cut the strips for the edging. Machine stitch these to the right side of the quilt. Fold the strip over the edge of the quilt, interlining, and lining, then turn under a $1/8$ inch hem and slip stitch it to the underside of the quilt. Iron to finish.

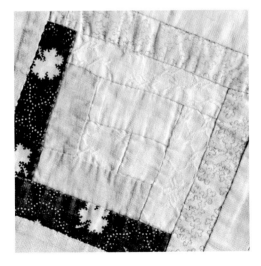

Antique log cabin quilts

This is almost certainly the most popular type of quilt, with hundreds of different varieties. You start with a square and then sew strips to the square in sequence. Back in the days of log cabins, it was popular to to have a red square in the middle, symbolizing the home, and then surround the square with lighter patterns on one side and darker ones on the other, symbolizing the sunny and dark sides of the house. Cloth was expensive and not readily available, so clothing scraps were saved and used.

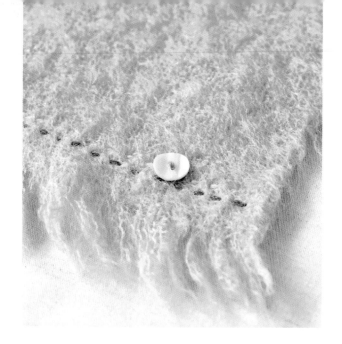

We all have throws and blankets and they offer scope for embroidered detail. Embroider a favorite line of text in loopy stem stitch across a blanket for the guest room, or add flowers to the part of a throw that lies along the top edge of the sofa. I found this large mohair stole at an antique textiles fair and loved its unusual pale mint color. A few months later I found a hank of hand-dyed wool in lavender and was struck by how well the colors complemented each other. It is worth looking out for hand-dyed wool in knitting shops because the strands vary in color through their length, giving a painterly effect to the embroidery.

Embroidered throw

Materials

A plain wool or cotton blanket with a fairly close weave

Wool

A button or two (optional)

For the template for the embroidery see page 134

Stitches used:

Stem stitch (see page 129)

Satin stitch (see page 131)

Running stitch (see page 128)

Method

1 Lay out your throw and work out how to position the motif(s) and mark the spots either with a pencil dot or a pin. To an extent with this project you are working freestyle because you cannot really trace onto a blanket. However what you can do is make a tracing with felt pen onto a piece of firm plastic. I cut up stiff clear plastic wallets for this purpose. You can then use this to make sure you are not veering too far from the design by holding it over your work periodically to remind yourself of the design.

2 It is important when working with wool not to pull the threads too tight and to keep the back really neat as it will be seen. The running stitch and button were added details at the last minute. Be careful about adding buttons if you have young children or chew-happy puppies.

At the window

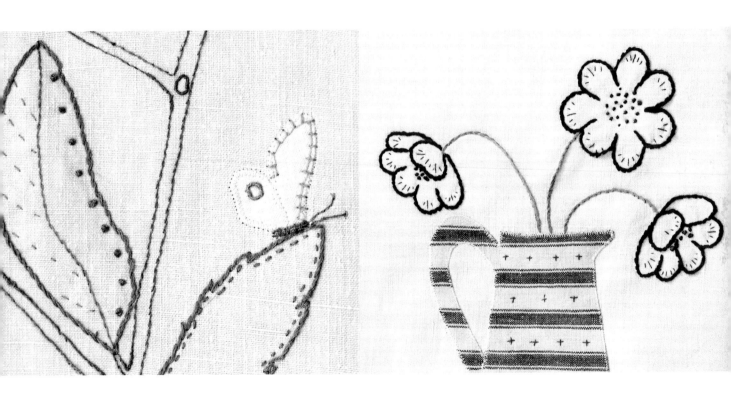

Windows, cupboards, and doors

Embroidering large pieces of fabric for curtains is probably too time-consuming for most people today. However, for a small window, or a window where you might use a roller shade behind a pelmet, you can create delightful embroidered curtains or pelmets. A more unusual idea is to treat glazed doors and cupboards as picture frames or windows, and fill them with embroidered panels. Fabric is often used behind glazed doors so it seems logical to create custom-made embroidery for the purpose. This offers an opportunity to create a piece of work that is either striking, such as the jugs in the panel below and on pages 124–27, or one that adds a subtle layer of texture to the room, such as the butterflies and leaves in the project on pages 120–23. Think about the room and make sure that the fabric and design you choose has the right tone and texture to work with the rest of the décor. You could even make special seasonal panels and change them through the year.

Left: You could fit your chosen design to the room it will be in, such as these cheerful jugs on a door to a kitchen (see pages 124–27 for instructions on how to make them).

Opposite: The pale green color of this Hungarian plate rack reminded me that I had seized upon a moth-eaten bed jacket in the same soft lettuce green in an antiques shop in Hay-on-Wye, perfect for the leaves of this design. The birds in this design are the same as those used in the headboard project on pages 98–101. Here you see you could work them using color instead of the white and lace leaves.

This is a good project for people who want embroidery in their home but do not want to do the embroidery themselves. Often customers tell me that they have piles of inherited table linen lingering in drawers, relics of a more genteel age when people used cloths on trays and doilies on tables. This project uses this type of vintage embroidery, so unless you have large amounts of the same fabrics, an exact replica cannot be made. The idea here is to let your creativity flow in finding and arranging the fabrics. If you prefer you could use the patterns and techniques in this book and embroider them in white on differently textured white fabrics to get the same effect.

White-on-white sheer curtain

Materials

A piece of embroidered sheer fabric big enough to cover the window with extra to create the scalloped edges across the top and down the sides. The advantage of using an embroidered sheer as the base or lining is that delicate tracery of the embroidery is revealed through the filtering light, adding another layer of interest to the patchwork. However, you can also use plain muslin.

A selection of white fabric scraps and trims—Think about using favorite old shirts with white embroidery on them, or lace collars, worn out pillowcase edges, or tablecloths. The only imperative is that they are white.

Threads—I never use white thread for vintage fabrics. I find a very subtle ivory works best.

Bonding web, enough for a piece the size of your window

Buttons (optional)

Velcro the same width as the window or café clips

Stitches used:

A selection of embroidery stitches to embellish the patchwork (optional)

Slip stitch (see page 133)

Method

1 Measure your window. This curtain is not designed to be drawn during the day but fixed with Velcro to the top of the window frame. The scalloped edges are not essential but if you want to include them decide how wide you want the scalloped edges at the side to be. These will be cut separately and seamed onto the patchwork at the end. Deduct the width of these from your window width measurement and cut a piece of sheer lining fabric with a $\frac{1}{2}$ inch seam allowance.

2 Lay your lining fabric on a flat surface. Assemble, wash, and iron your chosen white fabrics, some plain, some with embroidered detail. As an example, in this project I used the remains of a tattered tablecloth, the cuffs of an embroidered shirt, the frill of a child's summer dress, and a few old handkerchiefs and napkins.

3 Lay your fabrics out on top of the lining, trimming them to the size you want and overlapping them to ensure you have left enough for seam allowances, until you are satisfied with your patchwork arrangement. It is a good idea to include some larger pieces, and you may have one panel that you want to use as a central piece. If you decide to layer a scalloped edge across the top of the patchwork, as I have done, then don't use your best embroidered patches at the top of the curtain.

4 Stitch the pieces together. Press and trim the seams to within $\frac{1}{16}$ inch of the seam. You do not want to see seam allowance through the curtain if you can avoid it. Press the whole patchwork and lay it on top of the sheer lining to check it is the right size.

5 Now enjoy embellishing your patchwork. I like to oversew seams with machine appliqué. This adds texture and definition but also reinforces the seams you have trimmed on the reverse. Having stitched the patchwork together, you can embellish it with patches stitched on top, or by adding your own embroidery or buttons.

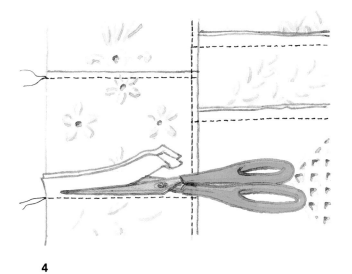

4

9 Now cut a piece of the sheer fabric the width of the patchwork part of the curtain at the top. Fuse it to bonding web and cut the scalloped edge out on one side. Fuse this to the top of the patchwork using an iron. Oversew the scalloped edge through the patchwork and lining with a small appliqué stitch. Now turn in the top of the patchwork and lining and slip stitch together. Stitch one half of your Velcro fixing to the reverse of the top of the curtain. Attach the other side to the window frame or a batten. You could also just use café clips as fixings.

6 If you have a piece of vintage scalloped trim (perhaps the frill from a worn-out pillowcase) or some pretty lace, could you use these as the side pieces. If not cut two pieces from plain muslin the correct width such that together they make up the width of the window taking into account your patchwork. Use the scallop template to create a scalloped edge along the outside edge of each piece. Press and hem by hand, following the instructions for the chair cover on page 53.

7 With right sides together, pin the scalloped sides to the patchwork so that the scallops face inwards and pin to the right side of the sheer lining. Stitch, turn, and iron.

8 Now either create a frill for the bottom of the curtain using the sheer lining fabric, or if you have a suitable piece of vintage trim you can use this. Pin, then stitch, right sides together to the bottom of the curtain. Press this seam open on the reverse of the curtain and oversew it from the front, using close buttonhole stitch. Trim the reverse of the seam right back to the stitching.

The word pelmet conjures a padded board jutting out beyond the curtains, trimmed with fringing: stiff, old-fashioned things. The pelmet in this project is more of a window hanging behind which you can install simple roller shades, as in this beach house kitchen. For this I have used up some of my favorite pieces of vintage embroidery, pieced with some faded blue-and-white check material. This is another project which makes good use of those pieces of embroidery you might have inherited or collected but do not know what to do with. Again, how the colors sit together is very important. If you want, you can embroider your own pieces, or as I have done here, simply add a few stitches here and there. Leave some spaces blank, though, or it will look too busy.

Vintage patchwork pelmet

Materials

A piece of paper as large as your desired pelmet size.

A selection of fabrics, some plain, some patterned, and some embroidered, uneven edges trimmed and ironed. It is probably best, depending on the effect you want, to use something quite soft and easy to blend for the patterned fabric so that the embroidery is set off, not lost. If you prefer to use a variety of patterned fabrics, try to keep them in the same color zone.

Backing or lining fabric

Interlining—you must pre-wash it so that if you ever want to wash the pelmet it will not shrink.

Buttons (optional)

Threads

A length of Velcro the width of your pelmet.

For the template for the scallop see page 142

Stitches used:

Running stitch (see page 128)

Stab stitch (see page 133)

Slip stitch (see page 133)

Method

1 Measure your window. Using the template for the scallop create a paper template for the pelmet. Remember to add seam allowances all around. The one in the picture is 12 inches deep from the bottom of the scallop to the top, excluding seam allowances. I find this is generally the right depth unless your window is particularly tall.

2 Lay the paper template, pressed flat, on your work surface. Now start to cut and arrange your fabrics over the template, right up to the edge, overlapping the pieces slightly to allow for small seam allowances. Work from the middle outward, balancing left and right as you work. Keep the area of the scalloped edge fairly free of embroidery. Stitch the patchwork together using overlock stitch and iron.

2

3 Cut the scalloped edge along the bottom of the patchwork. Use the template to cut the interlining and lining. If using Velcro, stitch one side of the Velcro to the top of the right side of the lining. Do this now so the stitching lines don't show through the patchwork. Remember to place the Velcro at the bottom of the seam allowance so that it will run along the top of the pelmet when it is turned out.

4 Lay the patchwork on top of the interlining, right side facing up. Pin together. At this stage you could quilt the interlining and patchwork together, using tiny stab stitches along the seams of the patchwork. This would secure it well. If you'd like you can decorate with running stitch or other embellishments, such as some pretty buttons.

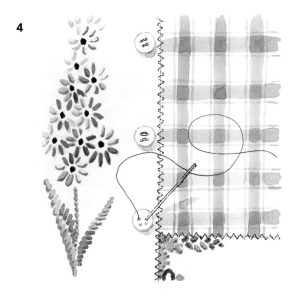

4

5 With right sides together, pin the patchwork and interlining to the lining fabric. Baste and stitch, taking care to make the seam along the scalloped edge nice and smooth, especially on the curves of the scallop. Leave a gap you can get your hand into at one end of the pelmet. Turn, iron, and clip the seams on the corners of the scallop. Slip stitch the two sides together at the opening. If using Velcro either paint or cover a piece of batten with fabric and use a staple gun to fix the second Velcro strip to the batten.

Using up leftover fabric

My workroom drawers are full of the tiniest scraps of fabric which I cannot bear to throw away. I bought the blue check fabric used in this project in France. It was lying in a crumpled heap on the road at a *vide grenier*, absolutely filthy with animal hair and feathers. It took three boil washes to render it clean. The blue would once have been a deep navy, but having spent a few years covering a cow in the cold weather the color had faded. If you make the pelmet opposite and find that you have little scraps of embroidered fabric left over, use them to cover buttons for a pillow in the same room. This is a fiddly job, but you can buy an inexpensive button-covering kit from crafts suppliers or haberdashers online which will make it a much easier process.

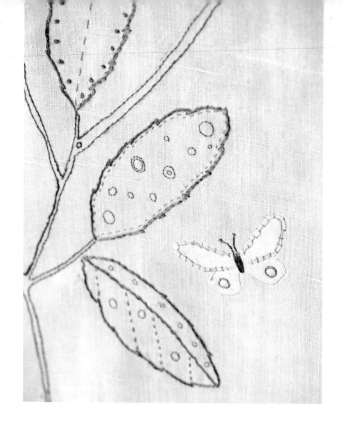

A year or so ago we visited The Walnut Tree, a well-known restaurant in Wales. The menu cover was a simple pencil sketch of walnut tree leaves and stylized walnuts and I was struck by its simplicity. I asked the owner if I might have a go at a variation and this is the result. It is a good project for practicing different outline stitches, and the design is one which you could extend to create a continuous pattern along, say, the edge of a curtain. One idea here is to create a family tree in stitches, embroidering a name on each leaf. You could also find different-shaped leaves in the garden, press them flat, and use them as templates. I like the design in green, but it would also look striking in gray or black.

Butterflies-and-branches cupboard panel

Materials

Linen base fabric

Threads

Linen for the appliqué butterflies

Bonding web

For the template for the embroidery see page 142

Stitches used:

Running stitch (see page 128)

Stem stitch (see page 129)

Satin stitch (see page 131)

Rollover stitch (see page 131)

Knot stitch (see page 131)

Slip Stitch (see page 133)

Method

1 If you are making this for a closet door as is done here, measure the open space and then allow a good $2\frac{3}{4}$ inch inch all around so you have plenty of room to hem and attach the edges. Mark the corners of the cupboard door on the fabric with pencil so you know where to work.

2 Make a template for the leaves and trace the design lightly onto the cloth.

3 Stitch the design. Vary the thickness of the threads and experiment with different stitches to create the outlines and veins of the leaves. I have used rollover stitch occasionally on the branches and leaves to add a bit of depth, and knot stitch as details.

4 Fuse bonding web to the linen for the butterflies and draw the butterfly shapes on the paper side using the template. Cut them out, fuse them to the panel, then machine appliqué in place. Decorate with embroidery.

5 Depending on how you plan to fix the panel behind the opening, hem the edges with slip stitch so that the edges are hidden when the panel is hanging. Attach the panel. Threading a short net curtain wire through the top hem and fixing the wire with two eyelet screws is the simplest method and allows you to remove the curtain easily for washing.

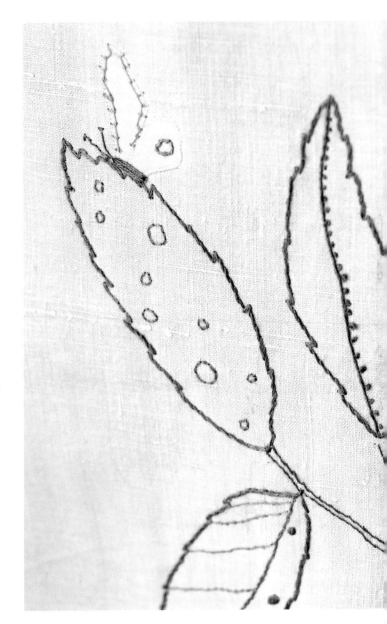

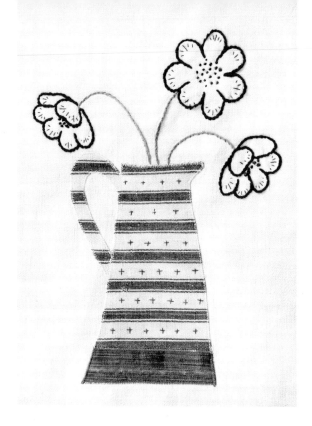

This dividing door with six glazed panels is typical of that found between kitchens and utility rooms. The owner of the house collects blue-and-white jugs so I decided to reflect this in the design. The embroidery is simple; stylized anemones worked in stem stitch using 6 strands for the flower petals and knot stitch for the centers. I made the jugs using antique French blue-and-white ticking, adding tiny embroidered details to each. However, if you do not want to do this you can just as easily embroider the outlines of the jugs (as seen on the placemats on page 69) and add further decoration. If you decide on this option use stem stitch worked with 5 strands for the outline and single thread for the detail.

Panels for glazed doors

Materials

Enough plain linen for a curtain to cover the glazed panel area plus enough at the top for a neat turn and to fix onto the reverse of your door, as well as a hem.

Lining fabric

Interlining (optional)

Fabric with which to make the jugs. I have used different French antique ticking in blue and white, but you could have a series of jugs in jolly floral fabrics or different colors. You could make differently textured white jugs and white anemones on a slightly darker background.

A piece of paper large enough to cover the glazed panel area with about 4 inches margin all round.

It is worth spending the time to paste or staple pieces of paper together to make this.

For the template for the embroidery see pages 142

Stitches used:

Knot stitch (see page 131)

Stem stitch (see page 129)

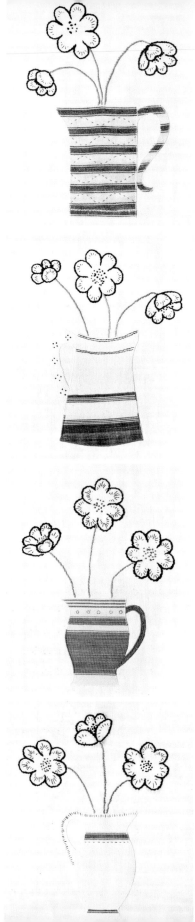

Method

1 Tape paper to the top of the door frame and mark where you want the curtain to be fixed. The distance between this mark and the top of the first glazed panel is very important to note, so that when you place the jugs on the fabric they appear in the right place behind the glass.

2 Pressing the paper against the door, draw around each panel to create a template of the glazed windows.

3

3 Cut around the edges of each glazed panel so that you have a paper template of the glazed part of the door with holes in it for each window.

4 Lay the template on the fabric on which you plan to embroider the jugs. Allow enough at the top for the fixing, and at the sides for folding back around the lining if you want to line the curtain (see step 12). Allow for a generous double hem at the bottom as the weight will help the curtain to hang straight.

5 Pin around the "frames" of each panel, then hang the linen against the door, holding it where you wish to fix the curtain and make sure that the pinned lines accurately delineate each glazed panel. Then baste along each outline to give yourself a frame to work within.

6 Fuse bonding web to the reverse of the fabric you are using for the jugs. Using copies of the templates at the size you require, transfer the templates of the jugs to the paper side of the bonding web. Don't forget to do this so that the jugs are facing the opposite direction to that which you want them to face on the finished panel.

7 Cut out the jugs and arrange them in the basted panels so you are satisfied with the balance of color and shape. Don't forget to allow enough space above for the flowers on their long stems.

8 Peel off the paper backing and place the jugs on the panels, then press to fuse them to the curtain. Do this two at a time, starting with the top panels. When all the jugs have been fused to the curtain go over the edges with a very fine machine appliqué stitch. Try to match the thread so that you do not get a harsh line, and don't have the stitch too large or too close.

9 Add decorative stitching to the jugs. I have kept this to a minimum but you could just as easily have plain jugs and add motifs from other parts of the book, although the charm of this project lies in its simplicity.

10 Using the outlines of the three different flower shapes, make tracings and transfer these to each panel. Enjoy deciding for yourself where they should go, then lightly pencil in the stems. Remove the basting stitches.

11 Work the flower outlines in 6-strand stem stitch. Work the veins of the petals in single strand and in a slightly different red. Work the black stamens in knot stitch.

5

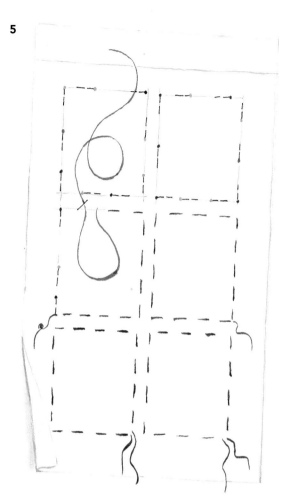

12 If your door is a dividing door you will want to line the curtain so that when it is seen from the other side you cannot see the reverse of your embroidery. Try not to use anything with too strong a pattern as it may be visible from the right side. Simply pin, baste, and machine stitch a piece of lining fabric the same size as your panel to the finished panel, right sides together, on three sides. Turn the whole thing through the right way. Turn under the raw edge of the open side and machine stitch to close.

If you are making this project for a cupboard you could simply fix the curtain to the wrong side of the door using a staple gun. It is useful to have someone on the other side making sure everything is in place

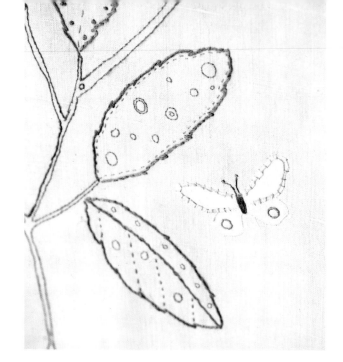

Outline stitches

Running stitch/Back stitch

Fix your thread at the back of the piece, bring the needle through the fabric and make a stitch of the length you want. Slip the needle back under the fabric and up again, possibly two or three stitches at a time, keeping the stitches and gaps even. Make the stitches tiny and close together for a broken outline; change the direction of the line to create paths or waves. To create an unbroken line use back stitch, working backward into the same hole as the previous stitch.

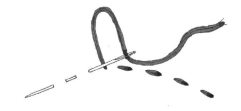

Stitches

I would like to open with a caveat: this book is not a book about embroidery per se but about using embroidery to decorate your home. My repertoire of stitches is tiny and self-taught, and I have no doubt that there are many readers who can stitch better than I can. I think of stitching as painting with a needle. So we have divided the stitch illustrations into outlines and fills. Some, such as stem stitch and split stitch, can do both. Think about the look and texture of what you are trying to capture in embroidery, and choose your stitches accordingly.

There are hundreds of stitches displayed in stitch bibles both on- and offline. Do not feel that you have to master lots of complicated stitches in order to get started. Just think of something you want to embroider, choose your colors and fabric, pick up your needle, and start.

Straight stitch

A simple stitch, which can be short or long. It can be used in so many ways: to make the simplest cartwheel daisy head, or to stitch blades of grass as in the bookend project. Fix your thread at the back of the piece, bring the needle through the fabric at one end of the stitch and take it back down through the fabric wherever you want it to be. If you look at the cherries in the picture on the bottom of page 55 you can see how straight stitch has been used within the outline of the cherries to give them more definition.

Blanket stitch

Traditionally used to decorate the edges of blankets, this is a curiously pleasing and versatile stitch that can also be used for appliqué, as in the daisy blanket pillow on pages 84–87. Bring your thread to the front of the fabric and then go back into the fabric about $1/4$ inch to the right on the diagonal and, without pulling through, bring the needle in line with where you went in on the left. Pull through, looping the thread under the needle, and repeat. Each new stitch secures and holds the loop of the previous stitch. Try to make the stitches firm but not pulled, and keep them as even as you can. If you'd like you can vary the length of the vertical stitch.

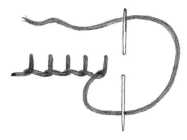

Split stitch

Split stitch was used a great deal as a fill in early medieval embroidery, working it in close rows to create subtle shading. Bring the thread up through the fabric and make a stitch. Bring the thread back up through the middle of that previous stitch, splitting it just before the end. It takes some practice but it is a lovely stitch. If you have the patience you can use single strand split stitch in very close rows to create incredibly fine textured fill. It can look like a very fine, elongated chain stitch.

Stem stitch

If you are right-handed you work stem stitch from left to right, keeping the working thread (i.e., the thread in the needle not yet used up in stitching) to the left of the needle or below the line of stitching at all times. This is reversed for left-handers. Strange though it may seem, if you keep the working thread to the right of the needle, you end up with an outline stitch that looks subtly different—a bit more like twisted rope. Start off with a couple of tiny stab stitches on top of each other which you will cover up with the first stem stitch.

Stem stitch is useful for creating elegantly smooth outlines around curves. You could use it for delicate edges, such as those of the leaves in the rosebud mirror frame project (pages 62–66), or in rows to create a textured fill. Like all stitches, varying the thickness of the thread will affect the look of the stitch. I used it with single strands to create some of the little birds in the nautical pictures.

Chain stitch

Bring the thread up at the start of the line and put it back through the fabric immediately adjacent to where it came out, but do not pull the thread all the way through. Holding it down with your non-sewing thumb is helpful. Now bring the needle back up through the fabric a little further on and slip it under the loop, pulling it back up the line. Keep your working thread below the needle.

Lazy daisy stitch

Effectively chain stitch but detached and can be used for flower petals and leaves to get a great and varied effect.

Vintage stitches

Vintage embroidery is very inspiring and can teach us more than any stitch bible. Even if the colors are not attractive, you can see numerous stitches and ways to use them. Shown here are several different ways to use lazy daisy stitch, from simple borders to intricately stylized flowers and leaves. In particular I like the way it has been used to stitch the spray of lilac in varying painterly shades, and the ferny leaves.

Fill-in stitches

Satin stitch

In some ways this is the most difficult stitch to master. Essentially it is straight stitch worked very closely to cover a shape. The trick is to create a very clean outline to work over, either by marking it with a sharp marking pen, or by sewing the outline first in a delicate stem stitch. In both cases you work the straight stitches so that they cover the outline. If you have stitched the outline you get a slightly more definite edge because the stitches underneath give a slightly raised effect. Do not pull the stitches too tight and remember that ironing can work wonders. If you are making leaves, it is quite effective to do a tight row of stab stitches down the center to create the vein of the leaf.

Knot stitch

I confess I cannot make sense out of all those pictures of French knots. So I had to invent my own sort of knot. I make two or three little stitches on top of each other to form a neat, smooth little mound and then go back down through the middle. It looks like a knot—although I admit that proper French knots do look wonderful.

Loopy stitch

This stitch may have a proper name but I have not found it. I just wanted to make my sheep look woolly without using knots. Take the thread up through the fabric and put it back through immediately adjacent, leaving a loop on the surface about $1/8$ inch long. Repeat and every 3 to 4 stitches do a little slip stitch at the back. Repeat until the area is covered. You do not need to make them all the same length—this is not about embroidering with a correct stitch but about using needle and thread to create a woolly sheep. When you press your work something magical always happens to this stitch and, frankly, I prefer it to French knots for sheep.

Rollover stitch

This is a form of couching, but instead of laying threads out and casting over them, you are simply rolling the needle over and over the line of stitching beneath to create a raised line. It is incredibly effective for adding texture to tree bark, masts, and poles of boats, and even to even out the odd bit of awkward stitching here and there, particularly on stems where your stem stitch might have slipped into a less-than-lovely back stitch.

Techniques

Stitching is like handwriting, unique to the person drawing the needle and thread through the cloth. Everyone who sews has their own repertoire of tricks and techniques and this affects the way they handle their tools. For example, if you work with linen, as I mainly do, you learn to manipulate it to keep the grain straight. I prefer to sew with my work lying over a cushion on my lap so the work is supported but floppy—whereas others cannot bear to embroider unless their work is set in a properly bound embroidery hoop.

Selecting needles

Learning which needle works best with different types of cloth and thread is a skill that is acquired through practice. A rule of thumb is that the finer the thread, the finer the needle, but you have to adapt this rule to take into account the tightness of the weave of the base fabric. I prefer to strip my stranded thread into separate lengths and put them together again as required, as I find this gives a smoother effect. I also prefer to prepare all the needles and threads before I start a piece and wind the threads onto card. Keep in mind that good stitching results from practice: the more you do, the easier it becomes.

Using bonding web

About a week before her wedding my sister-in-law decided to make tablecloths with appliquéd hearts and pulled in all available helping hands. I envisaged that it would be difficult to hold the hearts in place as they were stitched onto the cloths, but instead we fused the wrong side of the fabric for the hearts to bonding web, drew the hearts on the paper backing, cut them out, and then peeled off the paper. After placing the hearts on the cloths, we fused them to the cloths with an iron and the machine appliqué stitching was made simple. I had never heard of bonding web or done machine appliqué, but can remember thinking as I practiced on heart after heart that this technique could be used to make pictures, and I could barely wait to get home and try it out. It seemed to me that appliqué is treating fabric like a painted canvas, with the embroidered detail akin to shaded spots. If you use vintage fabric for appliqué

the effect is even more painterly because the fabrics are faded. The key thing to remember with bonding web is that you draw the object in reverse. So if you want your boat facing left draw it facing right on the backing paper. You can use bonding web only around the edge of a shape if you want the middle a little floppy and soft.

Using stab stitch

Stab stitch is not a decorative stitch, but a technique for hand appliqué. It involves drawing your needle through the thread from the front to the back for each individual stitch. It's a useful method for making very small fixing stitches, and I use it on very tiny areas of appliqué or vintage fabrics that are too delicate for machine work. I also used this stitch with the fabric roses (see page 65).

Slip stitching hems

This is not an embroidery stitch but an invaluable technique for hemming edges or closing gaps by hand, for example on a cushion. Start on the inside of one of the folded edges, cross to the opposite side slightly further back, and make another stitch, pulling the edges together, and continuing as necessary.

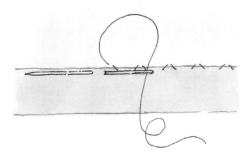

Machine appliqué

Essentially this is a zig-zag stitch, except that I prefer to take my settings closer to a buttonhole stitch. Set it as small as your eyes can manage and not too close or the effect is too satiny and strong. It is helpful to think of the needle coming up onto the edge of the fabric being appliquéd rather than the other way around.

Making buttonholes

If you need to make a buttonhole in a fabric that frays easily, you will need to do this with a sewing machine, following the instructions for your particular machine. If you are working in wool, especially felted wool, you can make a buttonhole by hand: it is just a slit edged with blanket stitches kept close together and even.

Starting and finishing

I prefer not to use knots for starting off but to make a couple of tiny stitches on the reverse and then proceed, with the same for finishing off. You can carry thread across the back of the work, but only if you stitch in the bit you have just done and repeat the starting-off stitch when you carry the thread over. Later you can snip the threads in between, confident they will not unravel.

Templates

You can use the templates given on the following pages by enlarging them on a photocopier to the size you require for your project. Make a tracing, turn the tracing paper over, and smooth the first tracing face down on a piece of paper. Now go over the tracing on the other side in pencil. With the right side up, place the tracing over the fabric so it is where you want your embroidery to be. Re-trace the outline so the pattern appears on the fabric, very lightly, in pencil. Do remember that you can also adapt and mix and match templates between the projects. For example, you may want to use the templates for the headboard shelf cover to fill a picture frame. Always feel free to add your own extra details.

Sheep and tree bookends (see pages 28–31)

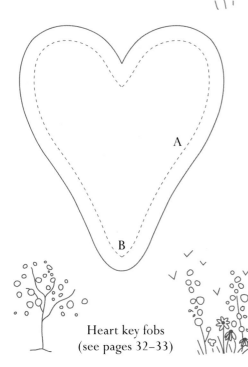

Heart key fobs
(see pages 32–33)

Daisy basket picture
(see pages 24–27)

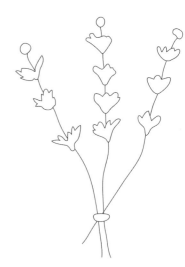

Embroidered throw (see pages 106–107)

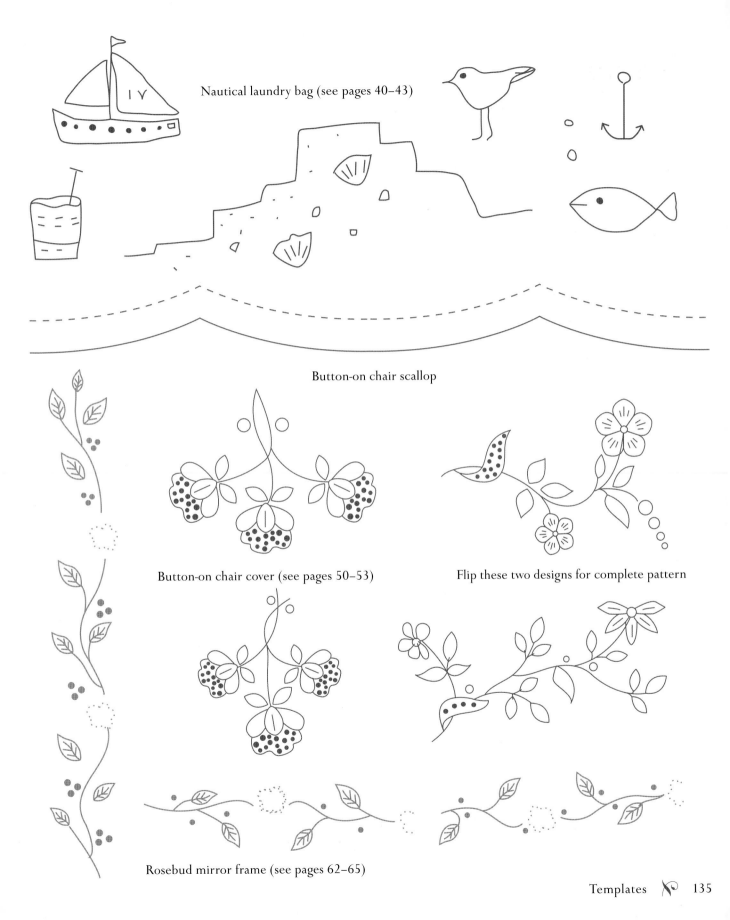

Nautical laundry bag (see pages 40–43)

Button-on chair scallop

Button-on chair cover (see pages 50–53)

Flip these two designs for complete pattern

Rosebud mirror frame (see pages 62–65)

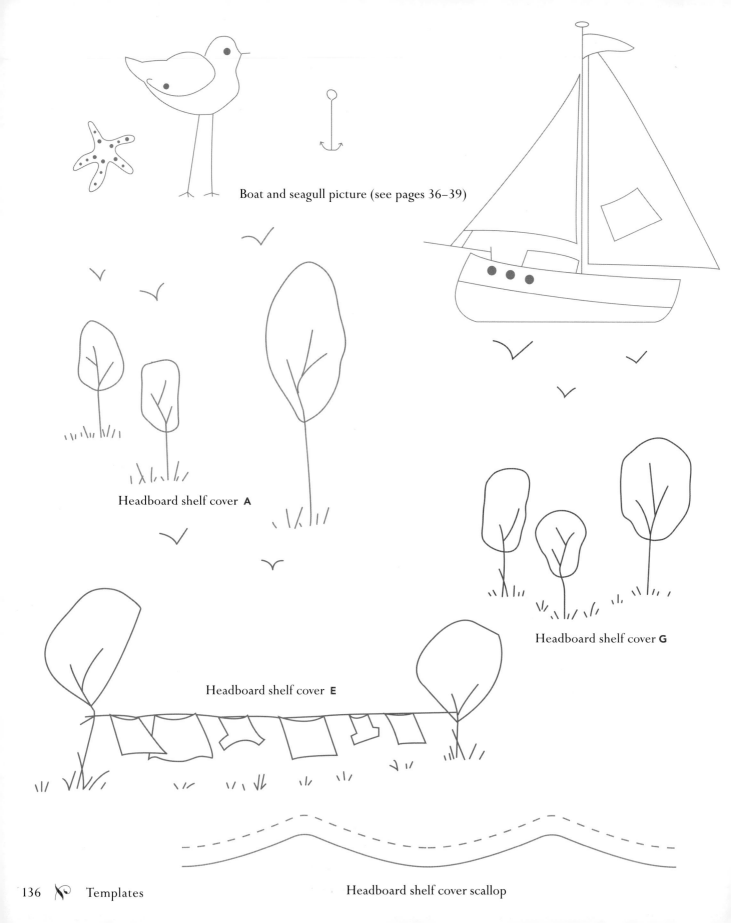

Boat and seagull picture (see pages 36–39)

Headboard shelf cover **A**

Headboard shelf cover **G**

Headboard shelf cover **E**

Headboard shelf cover scallop

A   B   C   D   E   F   G

Headboard shelf cover positional guide (see pages 58–61)

Headboard shelf cover **C**

Headboard shelf cover **F**

Headboard shelf cover **B**

Headboard shelf cover **D**

Templates   137

A   B   C   D   E   F   G   H   I

Kitchen shelf edging positional guide (see pages 56–57)

Kitchen shelf edging **A**

Kitchen shelf edging **B**

Kitchen shelf edging **C**

Kitchen shelf edging **H**

Kitchen shelf edging **D**

Kitchen shelf edging **E**

Kitchen shelf edging **G**

Kitchen shelf edging **F**

Kitchen shelf edging **I**

Kitchen shelf edging scallop

Pinwheel table runner
(see pages 70–73)

Daisy blanket pillowcase (see pages 84–87)

Egg cozy (see page 79)

Napkin rings (see page 78)

Placemats (see pages 74–77)

Director's chair covers – back
(see pages 94–97)

Flip the design for complete pattern

Appliquéd headboard cover
(see pages 98–101)

Harebells pillow (see pages 88–91)

Director's chair covers – front
(see pages 94–97)

Violet pillow
(see pages 92–93)

Butterflies-and-branches cupboard panel
(see pages 120–123)

Panels for glazed doors
(see pages 124–127)

Vintage patchwork pelmet scallop (see pages 116–119)

Suppliers

Vintage materials and haberdashery

All of the following suppliers were used for the materials and projects in this book.

Caroline Zoob
www.carolinezoob.co.uk
Hand-embroidered decorative textiles, vintage textile inspiration packs (including tickings, checks, and vintage embroidery), antique linens and decorative antiques, and homewares

The Blue Linen Cupboard
www.bluelinencupboard.com
A wide range of antique textiles and haberdashery

Dyeworks
www.dyeworks.co.uk
A wide range of natural colors dyed onto antique linens

The Old Haberdashery
33a High Street
Ticehurst
East Sussex TN5 7AS
www.facebook.com/theoldhaberdashery
Vintage fabrics, haberdashery, woodblock stamps, hand-dyed wool, vintage buttons

The Washerwoman
thewasherwoman.blogspot.co.uk
A guide to the best vintage and textile fairs, including the Talent for Textiles fairs

Donna Flower
www.donnaflower.com
Vintage fabrics and haberdashery with emphasis on retro style

Sewing equipment and advice

www.sewandso.co.uk

Stitchschool
Stitchschool.blogspot.co,uk
Very useful site with instructions for embroidery stitches

Royal School of Needlework
www.royal-needlework.org.uk
The School offers hand-embroidery courses for all levels

Artists' Materials

Green and Stone
www.greenandstone.com
Artists' materials emporium

Finishing-off

For those who simply want to stitch but get someone else to make up the project

Jose Miguel Upholstery
www.josemiguelupholstery.co.uk
Will undertake small projects such as mirror frames and bookends by post

Carved Oak
www.carvedoak.co.uk
Oak blocks for bookends

A Shade Above
www.ashadeabove.co.uk
Bespoke lampshades

Harper Crafts: Gorgeous designs, easy instructions

www.harpercrafts.com

Embroidery pour la Maison
More than one hundred projects you can use to prettify and personalize objects throughout the home—hand-stitched designs for everything from aprons to tote bags, bathrobes to notebooks.

Embroidery pour le Bébé
Ideas for more than one hundred projects to add charm to the items every new mother needs for her baby. Learn how to stitch designs such as teddy bears for blankies and zoo animals for onesies.

Embroidery pour le Jardinier
Personalize your gardening tools. More than one hundred projects reveal how to make everything from cherry motifs, to scarecrows, to pumpkins for items such as gloves, smocks, and seed bags.

Acknowledgments

First I would like to thank Jacqui Small and Jo Copestick for liking this book idea, and the editor, Sian Parkhouse, and designer, Maggie Town, for all their help and wise advice and for making this book such a pleasure to work on. The book would be nothing without Caroline Arber's beautiful photography and Kate Simunek's illustrations.

A huge thank-you to those who allowed us to use their homes for photography and for looking after us so generously, in particular Miranda Money and Chris Myers. Chris Sawyer proved himself an exceptional stylist's assistant on the shoots. I am grateful to Celia Pollington for her help with making some of the projects and to Karl Smith of Carved Oak for producing two oak bookends and to José Miguel for upholstering them and other projects at a moment's notice. Thank you to Woodpigeon, Foxhole Antiques, and S.J. Bennett Antiques for loaning props for shoots. Also to my friend Liz Allen for her help with some of the stitching on the door panel flowers when the 'flu had caused me to fall behind. I am grateful to Elizabeth Baer who has been a constant source of inspiration and font of knowledge about antique textiles.

Last, but never least, I want to thank my husband for tolerating the unexpected needles in the sofa arm and the general domestic chaos that surrounds deadlines and shoot days, and for always allowing me to pursue the things that interest and absorb me.

746.44 ZOO
Zoob, Caroline.
Hand-stitched home

$19.99

FINKELSTEIN
MEMORIAL LIBRARY
SPRING VALLEY, N.Y.
Phone: 845-352-5700
http://www.finkelsteinlibrary.org

OCT 1 7 2013